SERGE OUKRAINSKY, TODAY.

My Two Years With Anna Pavlowa

By Serge Oukrainsky

THE EMINENT BALLET DANCER

Translated from the French Manuscript
by I. M.

Noverre Press

First published in 1940

This edition published in 2013 by
The Noverre Press
Southwold House
Isington Road
Binsted
Hampshire
GU34 4PH

ISBN 978-1-85273-164-9

© 2013 The Noverre Press

Contents

CHAPTER		PAGE
	FOREWORD	IX
	PROLOGUE	XV
I.	RETROSPECTIVE	1
II.	SHORT SKETCH	3
III.	NEW HORIZONS	9
IV.	APPREHENSIONS	15
V.	THE FIRST LESSON	17
VI.	AS SPECTATOR	21
VII.	REHEARSALS	27
VIII.	FIRST DEBUT	33
IX.	OVERWORK	37
X.	PAVLOWA	41
XI.	IMPATIENCE	47
XII.	MONSIEUR DANDRÉ	51
XIII.	IVY HOUSE	53
XIV.	SERGE OUKRAINSKY	57
XV.	SECOND AND TRUE DEBUT	59
XVI.	CROSSING THE OCEAN	63
XVII.	NEW YORK	69
XVIII.	GENERAL HAPPENINGS	73
XIX.	PAVLOWA INTIME	81
XX.	CECCHETTI	85
XXI.	INCIDENTS ON TOUR	89
XXII.	THE STOLEN PART	93
XXIII.	GERMANY	99
XXIV.	CONTENTMENT	105
XXV.	THE DANCER T OF THE IMPERIAL THEATRE	107
XXVI.	PRESENTIMENTS AND OMENS	111
XXVII.	BERLIN	115
XXVIII.	ST. PETERSBURG	119
XXIX.	MOSCOW	123
XXX.	VACATIONS	127
XXXI.	PARIS, AUGUST, 1914	131
XXXII.	DEPARTING FOR LONDON	141
XXXIII.	LONDON	145
XXXIV.	OUR RETURN TO THE UNITED STATES	155
XXXV.	OTHER INCIDENTS	159
XXXVI.	MIDWAY GARDEN	175
XXXVII.	SEPARATIONS	183
XXXVIII.	INDEPENDENT	187

Illustrations

Serge Oukrainsky Today, Page IV.
Serge Oukrainsky in his famous "Idol" dance, Page 12.
Sketch of St. John by M. Dethomas; Serge Oukrainsky at the age of five, Page 28.
Program page of dance concert of N. Trouhanowa, Page 30.
Facsimile of the musical script and signature of Vincent d'Indy for his score of "Istar;" also of Paul Dukas for "La Peri," Page 34.
Facsimile of musical script and signature of Maurice Ravel for the score of "Adelaide;" also of Florent Schmitt for the score of "Salome," Page 38.
The incomparable Anna Pavlowa in her swan costume, Page 44.
Serge Oukrainsky in the "Minuete" by Mozart, Page 50.
The celebrated Dutch dancer, Andreas Pavley, Page 52.
Serge Oukrainsky in his celebrated Persian Dance, Page 54.
Anna Pavlowa in the "Dragon Fly," Page 62.
Snapshot aboard the S. S. Kaiser Wilhelm, Page 64.
The famous Pavlowa Gavotte statue, Page 68.
Costume sketch designed by Serge Oukrainsky for the Pavlowa Gavotte, Page 74.
Andreas Pavley in a perfect plain Arabesque, Page 78.
Andreas Pavley practicing under the direction of Cecchetti in a plain attitude position, Page 80.
Serge Oukrainsky in the ballet, "Oriental Fantasy," Page 94.
Clippings from the Dresden "Zeitung" and "Nachrichten," Page 98.
Sketch by Malvina Hoffman of Serge Oukrainsky in the Boccherini Minuete, Pas de deux with Pavlowa, Page 104.
Facsimile of a page from the Imperial passport of Serge Oukrainsky, showing the family name, Page 118.
Anna Pavlowa, Alexander Volinine, Serge Oukrainsky in a Grecian Pas de Trois, arranged by Ivan Clustine, Page 126.
Page from the program of Anna Pavlowa performance at the Metropolitan Opera House in New York, showing Serge Oukrainsky as both dancer and costume designer, Page 140.
Tamara Swirskaya at the piano, Page 148.
Tamara Swirskaya wearing a gown especially designed for her by Lanvin of Paris, Page 150.
Sketch of Tamara Swirskaya by the Russian artist, A. Iacovleff, Page 152.
Caricature of Pavlowa Ballet in "El Figaro," Havana, Cuba, Page 162.
Pavlowa with a partner in the ballet "La Peri" by Paul Dukas. Bronz by Malvina Hoffman, Page 168.
Program cover of Pavlowa Ballet, Century Opera House, New York City, Page 170.
Incense burner by Malvina Hoffman, representing Serge Oukrainsky in the Ballet Oriental Fantasy, Page 174.
Pavlowa in the file "The Dumb Girl of Portici," Page 178.
Serge Oukrainsky in his Persian Dance, Page 184.
Andreas Pavley as the Harlequin in "Rondo Capriccioso," Page 188.
Tamara Swirskaya in one of her terpsichorean interpretations, Page 192.
The five ballet positions executed by Serge Oukrainsky, Page 194.

Foreword

"PAVLOWA'S MESSAGE TO THE ART OF THE DANCE"

I regret very much that the younger generation never had the privilege to see Pavlowa dance—as a Parisian critic once wrote of her, "The Eternal Dance as was never danced before."

All great artists in all branches of art can be substituted, but never replaced. Through consistent study they master the technical difficulty required by the schooling of their chosen career and adding an individuality of their own, from a scholar acquiring the title of accomplished artists.

Pavlowa had the double advantage of having a grand personality, combined with a body made as if purposely for the career she selected. In addition she had endless perseverance and enormous resistance for her work which, all told, resulted in enabling her to become a justly merited celebrity.

The specialty of Pavlowa was, what is called in ballet terms, "Toe Work." Many times I have heard ignorant people explain "Oh! I do not like Toe Work, it is so stiff and artificial." To that statement I have to say, "Luxury begins where necessity ends," "Art also begins when nature finishes."

Art is not an imitation of nature, but an adaptation, a transposition to another key by the artist who is not like a reproductive camera, but who uses his intellect, his own conception to create a composition.

FOREWORD

The object of the ballet is intended to break all laws of gravity. The dancer must give the impression to keep his equilibrium indefinitely, also to appear to fly through space, consequently the dancer rises to Toe point in order to contact less of the earth as possible, creating the illusion of eternal lightness. This is the true purpose of the real ballet, and not to produce the circus stunts of agonizing toe exhibitions.

Pavlowa was not human. She excelled in these sylph-like visions. Pavlowa lived in a carefree epoch of prosperity when people could enjoy the colorful richness of the brush of Bakst. The light themes of the ballet were in accordance with the mood of the times.

By ballet exercises based on the experience of previous generations, Pavlowa trained her body to perform at will and her limbs she wisely accustomed to the principles of technique necessary for her style of dancing and also wisely broke the conventional rules of arm movements in order to give expression and meaning to gesture.

For her, dance was a religion, she lived to dance and had a horror of satire when the dance was marred to gain easy popular appeal which many dancers perform to camouflage their lack of technique.

Dancers do not really dance anymore. The dance today can be divided into four categories. First, the group of ballet dancers who believe that to be a better performer one must remain on toe longer, jump higher than the others, those who disregard beauty of line to give only an exhibition of boring gymnastic exercises, and have no real conception of the character or feeling of the dance.

The "Hoofer," whose principal advantage is to become a dancer within a short period of time. The only purpose being a rhythmical monotonous sound effect made by the feet, but without the beauty of movement, musical conception and interpretation of style existing in classical Spanish heel work.

The third group consists of Fans, Balloons, etc. For this dance

Foreword

the necessary requirements are merely to be a beautiful girl. This type should be rather called academic models in motion.

The fourth is what they call Modern Dance which these addicts have substituted for the natural school created by Isadora Duncan. This natural school was a comical paradox because if it is natural they do not need to study and if you have something to learn it ceases to be natural. In this school each one can be a dancer without exertion. The necessary requirement was to obtain a piece of chiffon or a flute and skip around to classical music and you were a dancer. But, this natural dance had the purpose to express mostly happiness and attempting to loveliness in accord with the epoch.

The modern dance is a continuation of that school but living in the time of depression, war and revolution. Their aim is to portray morbid prosaic conception and make ugly, grotesque, disconnected gestures without meaning.

Pavlowa's style of dance has scientific and mathematic principles when studied correctly, but with the modern dance so many teachers, so many rules.

The first performance of an exhibition of that sort was in 1913, the "Sacre du Printempts." This ballet meant to represent savage races and for that interpretation Nijinsky tried to reproduce the primitive movements that the human can conceive. In this A-B-C of ballet schools four steps are the principal foundation. One is to Plier in elementary ballet second position, the second is to raise the leg like a beginner with bent ankle; third, to lie on your back, and fourth, to jump with both feet in Kangaroo-like fashion.

If you can accomplish these four principal steps as in the natural dance, you are quite an artist in modern dance which is twenty-six years old.

These facts that I mention do not apply to Martha Graham or the Joos Ballet Company which shows ballet training, especially in their "Old Vienna," and which has original choreography.

These four conceptions are just what Pavlowa never did. With her every gesture, every movement had one of these two purposes:

FOREWORD

To give the idea of unreality as an immaterial vision suspended in space or a picture of harmonious Helenic line as an antique sculpture, or to make a movement in order to express an idea, a word, an impression, but never an unnecessary gesture.

In my life I have seen thousands of dancers, a few good dancers, very seldom a real ballerina, ONLY ONE PAVLOWA.

Serge Oukrainsky, Hollywood, California, September 1940.

I dedicate this book to the memory of Andreas Pavley, the great dancer and a great artist, who was my companion in joy and in sorrow.

Prologue

The idea had often come to me to write my memoirs. But I had always delayed, put it off, feeling somehow that only a special reason, an event extraordinary, could make me undertake the work of releasing this avalanche of stored-up memories. These had lain dormant, waiting to be written, but in this nomadic existence of mine, I had let time pass and these memories that had been so much in my heart, had been submerged in the mist of the past.

I regret not having kept a journal of my life. Written at the time of happening, things are naturally vivid, joys more brilliant, suffering more poignant. Time softens, effaces much, so that a diary to refer to would bring back the past in all truth. Memoirs seem to be the recital of a third person, of facts created out of an imagination more or less fertile, of a writer—but underneath these recollections, seemingly so extravagant and absurd at times, one can obtain the feel of real life.

I am sure that if some day I write my complete memoirs, the reader will accuse me of most fantastic fabrications. He will believe that I have followed the example of Benvenuto Cellini who, according to his story told, was beaten by his father with the single aim of making him recall that he had in his infancy seen a salamander disporting itself in the midst of a great fire.

Sometime soon I will write that book; for the present I will content myself by writing of my theatrical debut and of my two years with Anna Pavlowa.

This was my debut into a theatrical career and the commencement of a new existence for me. The two years I spent with her were, in a fashion, more anecdotal than profound or tragic.

I will try to recount briefly of the years and the events leading up to my story proper. To have a true understanding of the state of my mind and the way in which circumstances unrolled to finally place me beside Anna Pavlowa, this prologue seems a necessity.

EXTRACT FROM A LETTER OF MALVINA HOFFMAN

> New York City, New York,
> December 15, 1939.

How long it does seem since the good old days at the Century Theatre, but somehow all the memories connected with the immortal Pavlowa have a quality of immortality, too, for I recall with vivid accuracy all the impressions of those intense and exciting years when life seemed to be flowing along on a more peaceful river as far as world conditions are concerned, which allowed of more passionate intensity to be directed to the world of Art.

> MALVINA HOFFMAN.

Retrospective

I WAS born in Odessa, a city of Southern Russia, on the shores of the Black Sea. Of all the cities in the empire, this was the most cosmopolitan. Even in the time of the great poet Pouchkine he wrote of it in one of his poems thus: "There one already breathes Europe."

When I recall the souvenirs of my childhood, it seems to me that I must have lived in another cycle, so much all is changed for me—fortune, social position, family, friends, surroundings, country, aspirations.

Russia in these times had this particular, i.e., the faces of the rural people showed Mongolian blood . . . the churches, cupolas were Byzantine, the chants of the country—all these things had the Oriental flavor. By contrast, society spoke French and German fluently and later on, English. In the stores there were always those who spoke these languages and one could buy there the latest in European things such as perfumes and the models from famous Parisian stylists. Odessa had a large French colony as well as a German and Greek one. The city was founded by Admiral Deribasse, the Duke of Richelieu and the Count of Langeron. From a small Turkish village was developed a huge commercial port which became the Marseilles of

Retrospective

Russia. The arts were also cultivated. Odessa possessed a beautiful Opera House where Italian opera was mostly presented every season. There one saw the women of society in the loges exhibiting their family jewels and the very latest fashions from Paris.

Short Sketch

My family was of Hungarian origin, my great-grandfather on my father's side being a Hungarian Count, the last of his house. After Hungary was conquered by Austria, he abandoned his large ancestral domain, refused to become an Austrian citizen and expatriated himself to Russia, taking with him the family jewels and all else that he possessed of value that could be taken. Disgusted with the ways of the world, not counting on the family he later had, and not being vain as a true lord, he in becoming a Russian subject had his noble titles recognized in order to preserve the privileges of that class, but neglected to have his title of Count legalized, which resulted in the fact that his descendants, regardless of belonging to a very ancient family, had not titles attached to their crest.

A condition like this often existed in Russia. Some of the oldest families have no titles or very modest ones. Count Tolstoy is an example. He had only the title of Count, yet his family goes back further than all the Romanoffs. Again there are a great number of Georgian princes, princes of Bessarabia and of Caucasus, whose right to titles make those who really are of the nobility laugh, knowing that in those provinces merely owning two sheep could put one in the class of a prince. Their titles had no value until after the revolution when descendants of this so-called nobility commercialized them by marrying the rich parvenues.

My great-grandfather was attached to the Court of Russia as

Short Sketch

Physician to the Czar, and it was he who embalmed the Emperor Paul after his tragic end.

On my mother's side was the blood of Russia and Greece; she was also related to a King of Poland. All this mixture accounts probably for my complex character. My maternal grandmother was the widow of a General who had been Marshal to the nobility of the government of Kherson. My grandmother on my father's side was also the widow of a General, and she, by this position, had one of the principal salons in Odessa, to which came all the aristocracy of the city.

By certain alliances my family was also related to the great familes of France such as the De La Tremounille and the Montmorency. I give these details to explain my inheritance and the surroundings in which my father had been raised and which I, too, had in my youth. These things that have to do with wealth and titles have appeal, though based on artificial convention and human vanity. My father, after his marriage, lived in Nice during the winters but came to Odessa in the summer to be near his mother. So from my infancy I became a traveller, going and coming from Russia to France and vice-versa.

My grandmother loved to entertain. My father, too, was very worldly and forced my mother to partake of his tastes. I was left to the care of a nurse, then a governess, and later to tutors. Consequently I had very little attention from my parents.

This way of living broke up whatever friendships I might have had with other children and so did away with the normal joyous life of childhood. Solitude was the real companion of my youth and this rendered me timid and reticent.

In this life of balls and fêtes I was almost forgotten, and it was only my grandmother, whom I adored, who had any real affection for me. She died when I was ten. My father and mother separated, so I was face to face with the problems and enigmas of life at this early age. I pass quickly over my past family life to later years, skipping the annoyances which could impress upon the mind of a

Short Sketch

child of ten years. My father kept me with him. He built a Chateau on one of his Russian estates and also bought a home in Paris and completely abandoned Nice. Then to get me further away from my mother and my mother's people, he placed me at the Lycée Condorcet and later at the Lycée Carnot in Paris, pretending that it was better there educationally than in Russia. During summer vacation which was spent in Russia, his friends and all his entourage reproached him, saying that since I was a subject of Russia I should be educated in St. Petersburg, *not* in Paris. As a result he put me under the charge of a professor who made me go over in Russian all that I had learned in French in order to prepare me for a Russian Gymnase. If the desire came to my father to make a return to Paris, he instantly, to satisfy his own personal caprice, decided that Paris was the place for me to continue with my studies and thus forced me to drop my Russian studies. His way of doing was far from being beneficial to me in any way, I was retarded in my studies, deprived of my vacations and isolated from children of my own age. By nature quiet and reflective, I saw and was oppressed by the events that had taken place in my family and being in classes in Paris with children younger than myself, felt out of place, and had no chance to make real friendships.

In spite of all this, these handicaps, my father wished me to work with the aim of eventually entering the diplomatic service, a career which he saw would accord so well with his worldly tastes. He entertained at Nice, in the palace "Marie Christine" that he had leased, people of note from all over the world, the Enfante Eulalia of Spain, American millionaires, the Vanderbilts, Gordon Bennett, any number of Dukes and Counts and other titled people of France and elsewhere. So he saw in a diplomatic career for me greater horizons for his selfish mania of social events. It is curious that my father, who is really from a good family, has on that subject absolutely the mentality of a social climber and to have a conversation with him is the equivalent of reading pages of the Almanac Gotha. Because of an egotism and vanity simply inconceivable, he spent a

Short Sketch

tremendous amount of money on this outward show. These chateaus, palaces, fêtes, cost an enormous amount and although he had a very large fortune, there was a limit. So while entertaining the world most lavishly he would economize in other ways, and having very little affection for me, I was one of the ways. He gave me very little spending money. His keeping me with him and away from my mother was not due to any particular affection he had for me, but was to give the impression to the world that he was the perfect father; the faults were only on my mother's side. As a result, he succeeded in making my bashful character still more reserved and I had an aversion for everything which was hypocrisy, convention, social events, etc. On the other hand I developed great attraction for the art of painting.

Having too much pride to accept invitations without being able to reciprocate, I much preferred Bohemian life, where I could accept a simple *aperitif* and be able to return in the same manner, instead of dinner at the Ritz. At last, tired of living under these unpleasant and illogical conditions and knowing that it would be impossible to obtain my Bachelor Degree at the Lycée, I decided to come to a definite understanding with my father. I was fifteen at the time. He had many reasons to offer opposing my demands and caused a violent argument. But I firmly held my ground, insisting that I would not continue living in such a way, that I refused to be tossed back and forth from Russia to France like a parcel or a trunk, and that it was humiliating and I considered it ridiculous to be in classes with boys younger than myself, due to this perpetual changing. I said he must give up the idea of making me a diplomat, that I would not sacrifice my life to his foolish ambitions, give my time to a career for which I had no aptitude. That was my inalterable determination to become a painter; his response was that he would put me in a House of Correction. He had always used this despotic attitude toward me. I told him that I would not be intimidated by his bluff, that owing to his social position, connections, he dared not put his son in such a place, that if he really entertained such a thought I would appeal to my mother and let her know that I considered him absolutely insane and incapable of having charge of me. It is useless to relate what I had to go through before he finally gave in, realizing at last that he could not change my decision. I enrolled myself as a pupil at the Academy Julian's in Paris. My father had a private tutor at the house to coach me in other studies.

This curious situation of a rich orphan without money, yet having parents, made me more independent than are generally the sons of European families. The separation of my parents had advanced me in age; life held no secrets from me. Although a boy I lived as a young man, had mistresses, and there wasn't a theatre or a cabaret in Paris that I had not frequented. At this time I was really not unhappy; I had outgrown the feeling of loss for a mother's affection. There had always been a certain reserve between my father and me; he was only occasionally unkind now, so my trouble was just the state of being poor-rich. According to the laws of Russia, fortunes pass from father to son unless otherwise stipulated. All my grandmother's estate went to my father. My mother had her independent fortune, so I was at the mercy of these parents who had little affection for me. The terrible despotism of my father was unbearable to me. His having a very weak character would tyranize without mercy those dependent upon him. So my sole idea was for liberty—liberty. But how to become financially independent? I had a great contempt for mercenary people, but I wanted money so that I could be free.

My two great passions were painting and the theatre. Painting brought little wealth to those even more or less successful; I do not like water color and oil painting is expensive with canvas, color, studio material, etc., and I could not hope to earn a living and depend on myself during the years of work and study. The Theatre. But what could I do there? My voice was of a good quality, but not strong enough to carry in a large hall; however, singing did not interest me for myself and the *dance,* before the coming of the Ballet Russe in 1910, held no interest for me. I never dreamed of it for myself,

Short Sketch

moreover, I could not imagine that my father would ever consent to my going on the stage in any capacity whatsoever, and I could not conceive doing it without his consent.

I was not prepared for any vocation and I would undertake nothing that I could not do well. I had been feeling absolutely hopeless about the choice of a career.

New Horizons

THE BALLET RUSSE of Diaghilew arrived in Paris in 1910 and created a sensation. I did not see them. The best seats were too expensive and my social position would not allow that I buy the cheaper ones. With the spending money I had, I preferred to attend something that interested me rather than go to satisfy a purely snobbish curiosity. I was an assiduous attendant at the plays given by Sarah Bernhardt, Barthé, Réjane, De Max and Mounet Sully, Berthe Bady, Simone Lebargy. The plays of Batailles, Ibsen, Bernsthien interested me greatly. But the Ballet Russes of 1910 did not interest me in the least.

Then came a fête which changed the whole current of my life. Who would have supposed that a simple conversation at the table could completely change a whole existence?

My father gave a dinner toward the end of the year 1911, a dinner in honor of a Russian Countess from Moscow; she and her niece were staying at our house as this was the hospitable Russian custom. So it was to his country estate that guests would come and pass the whole summer season.

At this dinner were some of the social elite, some grande vedetes, and well-known artists, Lina Cavalieri, Nathalie Trouhanowa and Ivan Clustine. The conversation at the table was that of all dinners of this type. Things theatrical were discussed, the happenings of the day, politics, sports, the latest fashions, the coming Autumn exhibitions and of diverse other things. Suddenly, instead of being general, the conversation centered on Nathalie Trouhanowa and her plans for the season of ballets she was to give at the Chatelet Theatre the following spring. Nathalie Trouhanowa had been a dramatic actress in Moscow, but she had changed to a danseuse and was trained in this art by Ivan Clustine in Paris.

Ivan Clustine had been premier danseur and master of the ballet at the Imperial Theatre in Moscow and boasted at having been the instructor of Mordkin, who afterward succeeded him.

The Imperial Theatre of Russia trained their dancers in their own schools, the pupils received their instruction gratuitously, having of course been chosen for their talent. Following the training period they were associated with these theatres for a certain number of years, working their way to the top, taking examinations, going through drills as does a soldier in the army to attain the higher ranks. After the prescribed period of time the dancer was retired and received a pension from the government for the rest of his or her days. These artists, during the employment in the theatres of the government, could not be absent without official permission.

Ivan Clustine was in that position after having served for a certain time in the Imperial Theatre, that is, he had been receiving a pension from the Russian government. This did not interfere with occupying the position of ballet master at the Paris Opera nor with consecrating his free time to personal students, only to those whom he thought had real talent. He could do this because he was not dependent upon teaching for a livelihood. Nathalie Trouhanowa was one of these pupils. Ivan Clustine was now coaching her for these spectacular projects which she had in view.

The first year that Diaghilew came to Paris he brought with him almost all the principal dancers of St. Petersburg and from Moscow, the ballet from the Imperial Theatre, but soon some of the dancers deserted him. Pavlowa, for one, associated herself with Mordkin for a season in London and for a tour of America.

Ida Rubenstein, although she did not belong to the artists of the Marinsky Theatre, had appeared with Diaghilew in *Cleopatra* and

New Horizons

Scheherazade, but left him to create the St. Sebastian of D'Annunzio, to be played in the Chatelet Theatre, thus deserting the ballet for the tragic drama.

Mademoiselle Trouhanowa entertained the diners by narrating the following: She said that Diaghilew had brought with him a very brilliant company, technically fine; the stage settings done by Bakst, superb. But the music was a reproach. They had used, as example, for *Cleopatra,* bits from different composers, a Bacchanalle of Glasounow, a Persian dance of Moussorgsky, a waltz by Arensky and so on. The critics claimed it was not a Ballet Russe, but a Russian salad. There was also the ballet of the *Pavillion d' Armide,* the music to it being inferior. The ballets of the Imperial Theatres of Russia had conserved the traditions and the choreography and could develop the talents of their dancers, but while it was well to conserve traditions, it was lamentable to conserve the same old routine and many of the ballets were old in style and conception, with the exception of the new ones created by Michel Fokine, and they had best be eliminated. Diaghilew, being modern in tendency, recognized this and was creating new ballets as fast as he could to take the place of the out-moded ones of the Marinsky Theatre. But she, Mademoiselle Trouhanowa, was especially interested in French music and was planning to have a gala Musical Festival made up of only French composers. She planned to present four ballets under the management of Jacques Rouché, actually the director of the Paris Opera but at this time director of the *Theatre des Arts.*

These ballets were to have special artists to design the sets and costumes. Maxine Detomas and René Piot were two of the artists selected. The finest musicians in France were to compose the music and to direct their own work to be played by the orchestra "*Lamoureux.*" Florent Schmitt had composed *Salomé,* Paul Ducas, *La Peri,* Vincent d'Indy, *Isthar* and Maurice Ravel's *Adelaide,* which was of the suite of his *Valse Nobles and Sentimentalles.* These were to be given at the Theatre Chatelet, the theatre which had been the setting for the Paris debut of the *Ballets Russes of Diaghilew.*

SERGE OUKRAINSKY in his famous "IDOL" Dance.

New Horizons

Changing suddenly the course of her descriptions of these projects, Mademoiselle Trouhanowa began to lament about the difficulties of organizing these spectacles, principally because of finding the right partner. She said that there were many dancers but all nearly impossible. Some were only character dancers and had no notion of the ballet, others were classic dancers and in this case other difficulties arose. Often they had no personality, often they could execute the dance, but could not interpret the roles as artists; others again could interpret the roles, but they were badly proportioned, too short, too tall, ugly and so on. Then addressing me in the most direct manner she said, "What a pity that you are not a dancer! You are the perfect type for a premier danseur, the only one who could expect to be compared to Nijinsky." What she said, was it a blessing? A benediction? Or a voodoo? It changed my life entirely. I laughed and thanked her for the compliment, and said that unfortunately I did not dance, though I personally admired very much the position of an artist like herself; besides, I knew my father would never consent to my following such a calling.

A rather extraordinary coincidence was that my father had possessed a very beautiful baritone voice. He loved the theatre in his youth and had often played in amateur theatrical performances with Nathalie Kesko, a young girl of Odessa, who later became Queen Nathalie of Serbia. He had studied voice with the great Italian maestro, Lamperti, who was in Odessa and who believed that he had made a great discovery in him. He wished he would devote himself seriously to an operatic career. My father appeared in charity performances, some times with only professionals as fellow performers. He didn't know the worries and the troubles of this profession, having tasted only the social side of things; his friends made up the auditors, whose applause, though in appreciation of his lovely voice, was no doubt influenced by his social position. But my grandmother, who adored him, opposed his going on the stage. It was, however, his great regret not to have been able to follow this career.

New Horizons

My father, hearing my reply to Nathalie Trouhanowa, spoke up and said, "If it is your desire to become a dancer, I will not oppose it. My mother opposed my becoming a professional singer, and that has always been a bitter regret to me. I do not wish that you should have such a regret and reproach me later."

I took my father at his word, for I knew his changeable spirit, and answered, "Oh, then, that is different. I ask nothing better, but the difficulty is that your concerts are to take place in six months and I could never be ready in that short a time, and be able to do what it has taken others years to learn."

Ivan Clustine, the director of these spectacles, said, "If you are truly a worker and if your muscles are supple, and if you have talent as well, in six months I can train you so that you can fill the place of the premier danseur in the ballets."

"In that case, I accept with pleasure," I responded, and immediately made arrangements to see him the next day. He could put me to proof and then frankly tell me if I was fitted for this art. They then spoke of other things. Later we passed into the salons, but for the rest of the evening I was present only in body. My spirit was engrossed in the imaginings of a most fantastic future.

Apprehensions

SOME OF my thoughts gave me much disquietude. Would Clustine find me adaptable to the dance? Would he find in me the makings of a great artist? Or would he see in me just a simple Dilettante? Would I succeed in this art? Surmount the obstacles of existing competition and become a master of myself and independent?

At last the much awaited hour came. Clustine arrived. We began with a business conversation. My father, as I said before, gave me but a small allowance, not enough to allow me to pay for expensive lessons. I feared, not knowing Clustine, that he might be interested in me because of the prominence and wealth of my family. But Clustine, already receiving a pension from the Russian government for life, besides earning a salary as master of the Ballet of the Opera of Paris, was not greedy. In this that concerned me it was truly for him a question of art. Then again the desire to form a pupil who in his eyes could rival Nijinsky, for Nijinsky had not been trained by him. We fell readily into accord. He made me pass a minute examination which was very satisfactory.

When I was about five years of age I had taken during that winter in Odessa some dancing lessons from a teacher of the ballet, a Mademoiselle Midvedeff who taught in the social set all sorts of dances "de style," giving the fundamentals and elementary technique of the art of dancing. It had little value in this that Clustine wanted to teach me, but had been of immense value in helping my physical development. For Mademoiselle Midvedeff had impressed

APPREHENSIONS

on my infant mind that it was ugly to walk with feet turned inward, also that it was very ugly to be flat-footed and that it was necessary to point the toe to walk with distinction. Having a certain vanity, like all wealthy children, I retained these principles, loving intuitively all that was beautiful. These two points had enormous importance in this art which I was about to acquire. Having ridden many bicycles, my legs were naturally developed and were well turned out like those of a dancer, with supple muscles, not over-developed like one can acquire when receiving training in an inferior dancing school. Clustine, after having examined me as a buyer of horses examines a pure-blooded horse or a percheront, passed his judgment confirming the opinion of Mademoiselle Trouhanowa and told me that now all depended on myself, on my diligence. I had all things necessary for success. Every morning Clustine coached Trouhanowa for the coming concerts in the green room "foyer de dance" in the basement of the Chatelet Theatre. The mornings were reserved for her. Clustine told me I could buy my costume for practice and my dancing slippers at a well-known store, "Cray," in Paris. He then named the day for my first lesson.

I had the habit of rising late, often neglecting to take my walk in the Bois de Boulogne. I hated to leave my comfortable bed. So the first thing that I had to do was to *conquer* this habit. Having no carriage of my very own and living at the end of the avenue de Villiers, it was necessary for me to leave the house at eight o'clock, take the Metropolitan of the Champeret line and cross Paris to reach the Chatelet and be ready to commence exercises at precisely ten o'clock. This brought back to me my days at the Lycée. But *this* was of my own desire, and for this reason it was less disagreeable and it was with joy in my heart that I left that first day to enter upon a new life.

The First Lesson

IN MY first lesson, Trouhanowa and Clustine were both astonished at the exceptional facility with which I could immediately execute the very different exercises. My will to work and also my endurance surprised them greatly. At the Chatelet one of the loges of the artists served me as a dressing room and to get to the green-room I often passed across the stage. I cannot express how I felt in doing this, the impression it made on me. In my childhood I had seen fairy stories presented there, a custom of this theatre, and recently it had been the scene of the triumph of the Russian Ballets of Diaghilew. On these boards had trod Nijinsky, Karsavina, Pavlowa, and now I trod them. I could hear the plaudits of an enthused public.

In Europe much is made of the culture of the past and respect is shown to great artists. This is not so in America. Here mediocrity can be launched under the title of novelty and be received with acclaim with lots of ballyhoo.

It was with reverence that I traversed those boards. This new view of the theatre interested me immensely. True, I had been behind the scenes to compliment artists after their performances, but that was not the same. Now, it was in intimate fashion that I saw the theatre as of being a part of myself and my impression was entirely different. Returning to my first lesson—. From my study of painting, I had an understanding, an appreciation of line; having studied the works of the great masters of antiquity and of the

The First Lesson

Renaissance. So the postures of the arms used in the classic dance and the sameness of the poses affected me deplorably. I recognized the value of the exercises, but as to posture, I had my own personal conception. This caused Clustine to say that I had a grace particularly my own.

Every morning from ten to twelve, I was practicing with Nathalie Trouhanowa under the strict direction of Clustine. In less than a month he asked me if there was not some way we could arrange so that I could have a lesson, if I could stand it, in the afternoon at four or five at my house. We had in our house a large room which served as a storage room and where my father kept a monkey. Indeed, we had quite a menagerie: a monkey, a parrot and many dogs. I asked my father to give me preference over his monkey and let me have this room for my studies. He believed that my new vocation was nothing but a whim, and that I would never become a professional, perhaps appear in salons for charity. But he felt sure that in the end I would become social and accept all kinds of invitations. He agreed to cede this place to me as a studio; however, in exchange, I gave to the monkey a room that I had used for a photographic studio, and which I no longer needed.

After placing bars and mirrors in this large room, I had my own personal studio where Clustine came in the afternoon to instruct me. I worked furiously four hours a day and after three months an event occurred; it was the cause of much rejoicing to me and at the same time much disappointment. After a very difficult lesson, the execution of which enthused Clustine, he said he wished to talk to me seriously. I was surprised and asked, naturally, what agitated him. He said, "You have for the dance the greatest talent that I have ever encountered and more, you have the plastique to be a great dancer. It is for that reason I would keep you from appearing in these concerts of Trouhanowa."

I was stunned and could not understand his reason. I had worked so hard. Why should he keep me from doing what I so

The First Lesson

ardently longed to do? Then he explained, "For these concerts in the spring Mademoiselle Trouhanowa has no need of a partner, for in these ballets she alone is the star and there will be no opportunity for the dancer.

"When I began training you I knew neither your ardor for work nor your feel for the dance. I had judged but your allure and your physique. I had planned to train you so that in six months you would have been ready to dance in these concerts with her, but as we progressed I realized that I was in the presence of a young boy whom I could make a celebrated dancer rivaling Nijinsky. He is not my pupil. I have already made Mordkin; he is dancing now and had a great success in America with Pavlowa. But he is of a different genre. You are the only one that I have encountered who is in the same category as Nijinsky and my desire is to have a pupil of whom I can be proud and who will measure up to him. Now, this is my intention. I wish you to train for two years. In that time I can make you do what it would take six or more years to accomplish at the Imperial Theatre of Russia. Those concerts are to be very fine ones and to obtain future engagements it will be well, perhaps, to have your name on the program, if only as a pantomimist. You absolutely must *not* dance. I don't want you to appear as a dancer until I give my consent. I want the day that you appear as a dancer to be one of revelation."

I cannot describe how I felt. How happy I was to learn of the great hopes he held for me. But to wait *two* years. I had worked so hard to be ready and now found my real debut pushed further off into the future. Appearing as a "mime" left me no illusions as to the value of this appearance. But I had no choice in the decision. Clustine simply would have refused to give me lessons had I objected, and he was the only one at that time in Paris who could train me in the manner of the Imperial Russian School which produced many great dancers, some of whom were his pupils. He was considered one of the best teachers. One thing that especially

THE FIRST LESSON

appealed to me was to know that he objected to my appearing in society recitals as my father had hoped to compel me to do. So I agreed and decided to consecrate myself to serious study for the next two years.

As Spectator

I HAD completely abandoned my painting, my former passion, knowing that only the ignorant try many things, but accomplish nothing. I planned to concentrate all my efforts on the dance, for I knew it called for much work. I would keep in mind, however, the great works that I had so religiously studied but I would cease my frequent visits to the Louvre, whose every work, whose every picture, whose every sculpture, I knew so well. It was not that I had lost interest, but I felt that it was necessary to conserve my forces to counterbalance the enormous physical fatigue that my dancing imposed upon me.

All my days were taken up. I had only my evenings free. Those I would use as formerly and go to the theatres. But my choice of spectacle would be different. Only those en rapport with the dance would interest me.

The first ballets of Diaghilew that I saw were given at the opera. The program consisted of *Le Carnaval, Les Sylphides, Le Spectre de la Rose*, and *Scheherazade*. It was all in all a beautiful evening. The ballets were in demand. They were at their greatest popularity. It was worthwhile to see the house filled to capacity with a great number of celebrities. The artistic and the elite of Paris were there.

I recall, especially, that Ida Rubenstein who had left Diaghilew was in a loge *d'avant scene*. She was dressed in panther skins with an enormous bunch of white aigrettes in her coiffure. She radiated a subtle refinement with an audacious though eccentric artisticness.

As Spectator

My first impression of the Spectacles, the ballet *Le Carnaval*, impressed me very slightly. The setting, a simple curtain, as was used by Isadora Duncan, had at the top a large border, crushing too much the performers for me to appreciate it at its real value. I was so interested to see Nijinsky for the first time that it made me neglect the composition of the work. When Nijinsky appeared I realized immediately that he had a lightness absolutely exceptional. But in the interpretation of the role he employed a certain movement of the head which I had seen done by the Russian peasants in the dances which disturbed me as missing the refinement native to the character he was impersonating. What he was playing was of the *Comedy del Arte*, calling for a Latin malicious intelligence. The costume consisted principally of tights with the traditional diamons, but these were painted by hand and did not match. The tone of the color made it look as though it were faded, the effect being slothful. Although I recognized in him a marvelous dancer, my first impression was not at all favorable; I thought that his advertisements were greatly exaggerated. But Karsavina enchanted me. I found her very beautiful, and this is rare in a ballerina. I have noticed that the pretty dancers profit by their physical allure to obtain success and position, neglecting the hard work, and that those of less beauty perfect their technique in order to surmount nature's lack, and as a result become the best dancers. So it follows that the bad dancers are the pretty ones and the ones less beautiful become the ballerinas.

But Karsavina was a complete exception to this rule. Not only was her face very beautiful but she had not the least "embonpont"; she was light, elegant, refined with infinite charm and personality. Her costume of the Second Empire was charming. It was of white taffeta with designs of cherries. Her dances were delightful, ravishing. Bolm, in his "mime" of Pierrot, bored me profoundly. I regretted each time he came on the stage. The second ballet was *Les Sylphides*. This again did not impress me much. I thought, for this romantic period, a setting by Gustave Doré would have been more appropriate than this impression of Corot. The tarlatanes,

As Spectator

very long, worn by the dancers, "à la Taglioni," on the contrary, gave a charm of old etchings and most apropos of the tableau. They were a great improvement on the tarlatanes of the dancers of the Paris Opera. The aim there was but to please the eyes of the old *celibataires* in the front rows; it gave them a chance to gaze on the limbs of the dancers, but really gave them a horrible silhouette of the circus-rider ready to jump through the hoop on the back of a horse. The nude is beautiful and pure; the strip indecent. A beautiful form, nude, posing in an artists' studio can inspire a work of art. An artist of the theatre in a costume suggestive, but of good taste, exotic, can be very attractive as can be a chorus girl in the Follies Bergere in a costume suggestive and licentious, but these short tarlatanes are monstrosities created by a libertine in thought. I am shocked every time I see one, not by the pornographic hypocritical intention, but for the bad taste displayed.

Les Sylphides is a ballet of the old school, traditional, classic, but through the genius of Michel Fokine had been made most interesting. The group arrangement was admirable and its execution in 1911 was irreproachable. Karsavina charmed anew. I was agreeably surprised by Nijinskaya, who employed a virtuosity remarkable, and at that time they had not talked enough about her. Nijinsky pleased me more, for he created an atmosphere of poise and romanticism in this role he interpreted. He also had some very beautiful gestures, but I could not see why he repeated the same steps that he used in *Le Carnaval*. I felt that he should have shown more of a contrast in impersonating a harlequin, or a poet.

Le Spectre de la Rose was the third tableau. My first impression was of the settings by Bakst. It showed him to be a consummate artist. He had designed it with a ceiling very low, and the furniture also low to the floor. The whole set was done as if to intensify the lightness and the elevation of Nijinsky. This was a masterpiece of optical illusion. Karsavina again filled me with admiration, like delicate porcelain she appeared fragile. Her visage was finely outlined like a cameo and her play so charming that the

As Spectator

memory of it is unforgettable. Nijinsky made his much publicized entrance through the window. I was rather in a prejudiced mood against him, as I never liked to be led by advertising and general opinion. It was not only the athletic jump that I admired, but the way he conserved in the leap, the most beautiful lines of the dancer. In reading the story of *Le Spectre de la Rose* in the reviews before having seen it, I believed that Nijinsky represented the flower itself, but this was not so. It was not just as the futile appearance of a flower, it was as the apparition, ardent, of the lover appearing in the likeness of the rose that he had given to her in the dawn of their love, according to the poem of Théoplyle Gautier. After the marvelous entrance, he vaulted here and there on the scene and then passed as if in the air behind the chair of the sleeping Karsavina, then abandoning the banal postures of the arms used in the conventional ballet, he took some postures recalling to my mind those of the *Slave* of Michel Angelo. Then again changing, he gave a series of the most beautiful attitudes. Nijinsky had a body curiously proportioned, but withal harmoniously balanced. One would believe that his limbs belonged to another person, the legs were very strong and his neck was very heavy. These two characteristics did not detract from the general estheticism of his person, but gave him great individuality and the power to hold his poses more sculpture-like. It seemed to me strange that the press and the public naivete enthused only on his leaps, ignoring his poses which to me were the most beautiful phase of the composition.

Karsavina awakens from her dreaming, rises, and with him dances the glorious "pas de deu" composing this ballet. I was enthusiastic over this spectacle and felt that Nijinsky and Karsavina had not been given praise enough, and thought that their talent had not yet been fully discerned. Personally, I can say that *Le Spectre de la Rose,* executed by Nijinsky and Karsavina, was one of the most perfect ballets that I have ever seen presented. It has been truly a veritable annoyance to me in later years to see this masterpiece

As Spectator

interpreted by mediocre dancers using of the original only the title and the music on which it was composed.

Scheherazade terminated the spectacle. It also enthused me on the moment. Before all else, the Bakst decorations charmed my eyes. Abandoning the usual conception of an Oriental setting, always so suggestive of the Hamman Baths or the stores de la place Clichy, he drew on his imagination, getting inspiration from the tales of the *One Thousand and One Nights,* even exaggerating their oriental spirit. With broad strokes of much color he gave a scene expressing the quintessence of exoticism. I seemed almost to sense the aroma of the Orient as I remembered it from my short stay once in Constantinople. Michel Fokine again demonstrated his ingeniousness and originality in his choreography.

Karsavina, this time, seemed too "usual," not strange or bizarre enough. She was too much ballerina. I should have preferred to have seen in the role Ida Rubenstein, Sarah Djely, Fokina or Ruth St. Denis. Nijinsky again made a beautiful creation, but I much regretted that he had appeared in the four ballets. It would have been better if the program had been so arranged as to give him more time to have a better "make-up". His face was so daubed with black that it gave him more the appearance of a chimney-sweep than of a savage negro and a favorite lover. He did some steps that he had performed in *Carnaval* and *Sylphides.* It surely would have been better artistically if the contrasts in the roles had been more definitely drawn. Personally, it would have been more to my taste to see Nijinsky truly representing a harlequin, a poet, or a Negro, than to see the perfect execution of the classic ballet with Nijinsky merely dressed in the costume of these different characters. But then again his flight at the end of his death was very well conceived; he had entered fully into the role he portrayed.

On coming out of the opera, I thought of the very beautiful spectacles I had seen. I was filled with admiration for Bakst, recognizing in him the originator of an entirely new mode of theatrical decoration. Michel Fokine, too, I saw had broken away from the

As Spectator

"already done," coming out of the rigidity of the old ballet and extending its conventional limits. He, by his new conceptions, was creating a new horizon.

Nijinsky was a brilliant dancer and a great artist, having not only exceptional elevation, but also a thing that was very great, a conception of the plastique which demonstrated so gloriously the stupidity of the old Italian school where girls were used for male parts. Karsavina was a dancer, the finest, full of delicate femininity, beautiful and extremely musical.

Rehearsals

THE SPECTACLES of Diaghilew did not discourage me in my own work. Instead, they filled me with the ambition to more quickly attain to their standard. All the great arts have this in common, that all are very difficult to realize and when well done must give the effect of simplicity, of ease. Terpsichore differs not from her sister arts in this, and the ballet, her legitimate offspring, submits to these traditional rules. The art of the dance is to camouflage the difficulties of its execution. A dancer, showing effort, is not a finished product, but only a pupil making the steps, having neither personality nor mastery of the technique of his art.

It is not the same for the *enfants* of adoption of terpsichore, jazz and the tap, or acrobatic, dancing. These are not art, truth to say. The aim of the circus is but to make the difficulties more evident for the edification of the public and not try to hide the odious lines of its execution. It is for this reason the classic ballet is discouraging to many of her would-be disciples, for those who are without perseverance cannot succeed, and few, before entering, realize the difficulties to be surmounted. The failures, then, in this line invariably take up some dance less difficult, created by a new school, the name of which, generally pompous, serves but to disguise their laziness or their incapacity.

My desire to become independent of my father and the horror I had of being mediocre, gave me a superhuman force. I had it in my head, or rather Clustine had put it into my head, that I must

Serge Oukrainsky at the age of five, with his grandmother at Odessa, Russia.

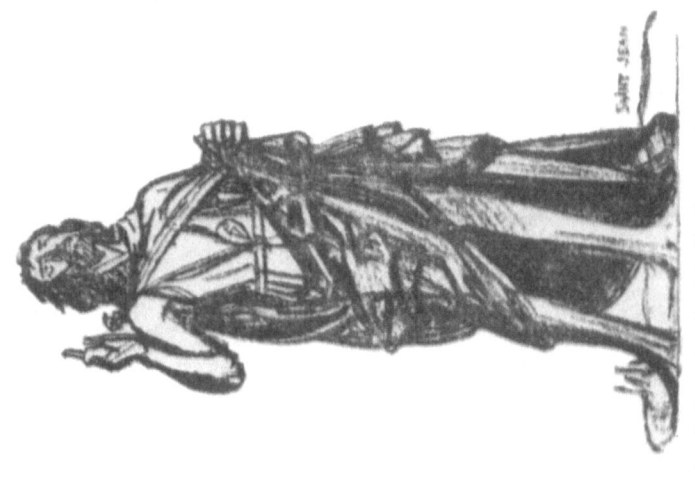

Sketch of St. John by M. Dethomas, from "La Tragedie De Salome," role played by Serge Oukrainsky.

equal Nijinsky. I said, to equal, not to resemble him, for in spite of my great admiration for him and the inspiration he had been to me many times, I desired to be myself. This, too, is common to all the arts: that an artist must be individual. He can be inferior, equal, or superior to his master or model, but to resemble or to imitate him he becomes then only a copy of the original and as such automatically becomes inferior.

The two periods most difficult to surmount are the beginning, when one must learn the fundamentals, and the end, when one must abandon what he has learned at the school and branch out creating his own style. It is at this period that the dancer can quit his appelation of student and become clothed with the title of artist. No one can explain or direct this last step, for it is the dancer himself who must discover his new domain, and so form his new line according to his talents, his inclinations, his inspirations and his individuality. Few good dancers reach that point, and this is also the universal law in every art. It is only then that one can have a certain contentment. But, at this time, I was still too far away from this period to demand or realize just how I was to develop.

As it had been decided that I would be only a "mime" in these spectacles of Trouhanowa, Clustine started to give me lessons in pantomime. On these occasions it was necessary for me to use the utmost diplomacy so as not to offend him. He and Cecchetti were recognized in Russia as the greatest teachers of ballet, and Clustine was in this respect, a marvelous instructor, especially when he took a personal interest in a pupil. But I knew that for pantomime Clustine was demode, impossible and infantine in his conceptions. I had assiduously gone to see the best actors and actresses play in Paris, and had formed an opinion on what to do and what not to do in the interpretations of different emotions in various roles, so I recognized his lack as an instructor in this line. How to get out of this predicament without hurting him and without loss of time, worried me. Happily I discovered a way which succeeded infallibly. If Clustine commenced a lesson in pantomime, I would ask him if he would again

CONCERTS DE DANSE

DONNÉS PAR Mᵐᵉ

N. TROUHANOWA

SOUS LA DIRECTION DE MM.

Vincent d'INDY — Florent SCHMITT
Maurice RAVEL — Paul DUKAS

AVEC LE CONCOURS DE L'ORCHESTRE DE L'ASSOCIATION DES
CONCERTS LAMOUREUX

Chorégraphies réglées par le Maître de Ballet de l'Opéra
M. IVAN CLUSTINE

ISTAR   Vincent d'Indy

Sous la direction de l'auteur

Istar : .... Mᵐᵉ TROUHANOWA
Le fils de la vie .... M. de CARVA
Les sept gardiens : MM. VANDELEER, BERGER, FRAISSET, SCHWARTZ,
                        DESCLAUZAS, RECAT, PIERI.

Décor et Costumes de M. George Desvallières

LA PÉRI (première audition)   Paul Dukas

Sous la direction de l'auteur

La Péri .... Mᵐᵉ TROUHANOWA
Iskender .... M. BEKEFI
                                         de l'Opéra Impérial de St-Pétersbourg

Décor et Costumes de M. René Piot

LA TRAGÉDIE DE SALOMÉ   Florent Schmitt

D'après M. Robert d'Humières. — Sous la direction de l'auteur.

Salomé .... Mᵐᵉ TROUHANOWA
Hérodias .... Mᵐᵉ NEITH-BLANC
Hérode .... M. JACQUINET
Jean .... M. de CARVA
Gardes : MM. BERGER, PIERI.
Les Voix : Mᵐᵉˢ VUILLEMIN, LABARTHE, CHADEIGNE.
Suivantes et Musiciennes : Mᵐᵉˢ RIDDE, TENSI, VIENNOIS, BORCKHEIM,
    C. DEBLIKER, GUILLAUMIN, BALDY,
    TOLINI, PONS, G. DEBLIKER BEAUDRIER.

Décor et Costumes de M. Maxime Dethomas

ADÉLAIDE ou le Langage des fleurs
d'après "les Valses nobles et sentimentales"
                                          Maurice Ravel

(première audition) sous la direction de l'auteur

Adélaïde .... Mᵐᵉ TROUHANOWA
Lorédan .... M. BEKEFI
                                         de l'Opéra Impérial de St-Pétersbourg
Le Duc .... M. VANDELEER
Les invitées : Mᵐᵉˢ RIDDE, TENSI, VIENNOIS, BORCKHEIM,
    C. DEBLIKER, GUILLAUMIN.
Les invités : MM. BERGER, FRAISSET, SCHWARTZ, DESCLAUZAS,
    RECAT, PIERI.
Le domestique : M. MICHELET.

Décor et Costumes de M. Drésa

Répétiteur M. MARSEILLAC

Program page of dance concert of N. Trouhanova. Serge Oukrainsky appearing under his family name of de Carva in "Istar" and "La Tragédie de Salomé".

[30]

explain to me a certain step of dance that I had had in the preceding lesson, which I explained I hadn't quite grasped. This he would do and would show me other examples in his demonstrations. Then following along that line, he would become so interested that he would cite another and still another so my lesson in pantomime was suddenly changed to a regular lesson *de ballet*.

As the time for the spectacles of Trouhanowa approached we had rehearsals and dress rehearsals. As "mime," I was to be in but two ballets. One was *Istar*, which Trouhanowa portrayed and in which I had the role of *Fils de la Vie*, her lover. The other was *Salomé*, in which I portrayed *St. John the Baptist*.

For the ballet *La Péri*, and also for *Adélaide*, *The Language of the Flowers*, Trouhanowa had a dancer from London, a Russian by the name of Bekefi.

For the role of *Herod* in the spectacle of *Salomé*, a notable *mime* was engaged by Trouhanowa. We had an important part to play together. Clustine staged this ballet and was so engrossed in this dance that he was absolutely lost to us, directing our pantomime spasmodically and showing us continually different things to do without any meaning. This "mime," Monsieur Jacquinet, took me aside and said, "We cannot continue this way and appear. Clustine never shows us how to do the same thing twice in the same way. Let us direct ourselves, Monsieur. Would you mind?" I was only too happy to agree to this and complimented myself on having always evaded these lessons in pantomime of Clustine's. So, holding to the things of Clustine's which we could use so as not to offend him and adding our own, we studied it out. Fortunately for us, Clustine had his hands full directing the four ballets and accepted our arrangement as a happy collaboration. I gave a sigh of relief, glad that he took it in that spirit and with such good grace.

I was not nervous over my role in *Istar*, being a very minor part, having played much *des comedies de salon*. At the costumers I found myself in my element, and no one suspected that I was a debutant. Two things occurred that gave me much encouragement.

Rehearsals

The "Café Neopolitan" was, at this time, the rendezvous for journalists and critics of the press at the hour of the aperitif. A friend of mine, an artist, was much with this group, and he told me that in speaking of the future concerts of Trouhanowa they said that she had a marvelous dancer with whom she trained each morning under the tutelage of Clustine. This gave me much pleasure, that even before appearing my work was being praised. The other nice thing was that during the dress rehearsals in the *Fils de la Vie* one of the ballet girls asked if my figure was really natural or given its effect by some theatrical subterfuge. She praised my physique; this amused me greatly and gave me the hope to not be ignored.

First Debut

AT LAST the day of the Spectacles arrived. It was well that I had little to do, my emotion was so great. To appear the first time in public before the critics of the press, before the elite of society, before the artistic and the worldly of Paris, in a great gala of dance with one of the best orchestras, under the baton of the principal composers of France, would have given a certain thrill to the most blasé. But for a debutant like me the sensation was tremendous.

I was the first to arrive at the theatre. Fearing that traffic or an accident might somehow cause a delay, I applied my makeup as I had for general dress rehearsal, happy in the fact that the artist that had designed the decorations and the costumes, Mixime Dethomas, had given his approbation as to the way in which I had done it. I had striven to reproduce the emaciated visage of the *St. John of Donatello,* which had always impressed me and stayed in my memory since I had seen and admired him in Florence. En scene, I waited impatiently the lifting of the curtain during the beautiful overture of *Salomé* by Florent Schmitt. The decorations were simple of line and sombre in aspect, giving the atmosphere of the tragedy about to be enrolled. The conception of the costumes was in accord with the drama. Salome's alone was not pleasing to me. Dethomas holding that Judea, being under Roman influence at the time, a princess of that country would have been influenced by the mode of that period. Therefore, he dressed *Salomé* à la Roman. The most beautiful *Salomés* I have even seen were by Gustave Moreau, who had painted

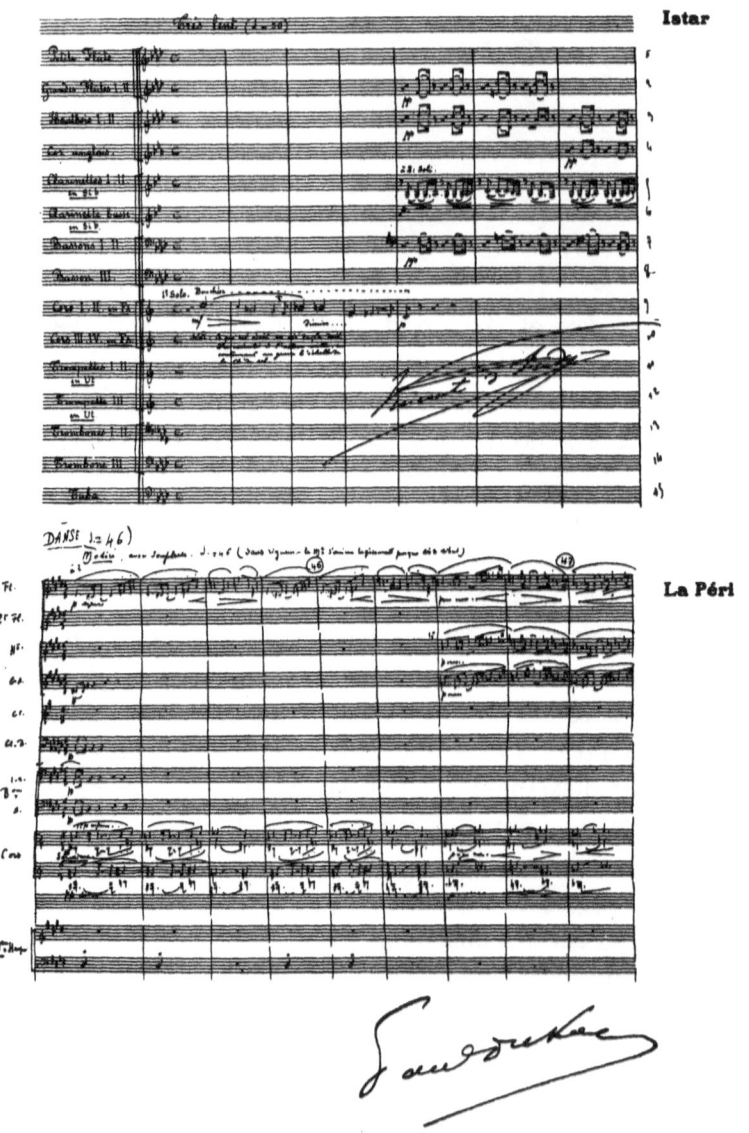

Facsimile of the musical script and signature of Vincent d'Indy for his score of "Istar".
Also of Paul Dukas for "La Peri".

First Debut

them seductively, exotic, strange and perverse, not of a style very definite, but essentially oriental in aspect, symbolically voluptuous, cruel and fatal like those that are in the museums of Gustave Moreau and in the Museum of Luxenbourg.

At last the curtain lifted and the brilliance of the lights, the sensation of thousands of eyes directed towards me, had the effect on me as having drunk many glasses of champagne. I acquitted myself creditably and came off the stage with a feeling that all had passed without incident. I believed sincerely that I had made my real debut.

For the second ballet, my entrance was at the end instead of the beginning. This poem, *Istar,* had for its music the marvelous work of Vincent d'Indy, a great master and a charming man. When the door opened through which I was to make my entrance on to the scene with all the electrical projectors focused on me and the throbbing chords of the music representing the resurrection of *Fils de la Vie,* I seemed to be really reborn, to be entering a life entirely new. The applause was tumultuous but it left me cold, for I knew it was meant not for me, but for Mademoiselle Trouhanowa. My part was too small to merit attention. I devoutly wished the day to arrive when I would be receiving a like reception.

The ballet of *Adélaide,* or *The Language of the Flowers,* interested me but moderately. I admire Ravel much as a great musician and having made his acquaintance realized in him a very amiable man, but this music is not one of his best works and, moreover, it had not been conceived as a ballet.

All my attention was directed on the *La Péri* of Ducas, of which the music and then the story entranced me. I would have much loved to interpret it in a style absolutely symbolic, mystic. It is strange that regardless of being a beginner this ballet received my influence. It is written in the story that Ischander, having lost the flower of immortality, returned sadly to the world of men. I expressed to Clustine how I regretted, above all, not being able to interpret this ballet. I explained to him what I thought would be a

First Debut

preferable termination. Clustine admired enormously my interpretations and paid me the compliment of having the end of the libretto changed to conform to my idea.

After the "premier spectacle," the other three following did not give me the same sensation. The papers were filled with eulogies, especially for Trouhanowa, for the composers, the artists, painters and the choreographers, but not for me; only my name was mentioned. I could not have hoped for myself, as the parts which I had interpreted were of such little importance.

Overwork

Thus, I made my debut. And truth to say, I was no more advanced than before. I recommenced assiduously my training but though my will and tenacity were resolute, my physique was not so strong and the fatigue of the muscles of my legs was such that I walked, limping. At the commencement of each lesson, I had to overcome the most excruciating pains by limbering and warming up with the barre exercises, although when finished the pains returned with renewed vigor. I was obliged to consult a doctor. He prescribed rests and injections of arsenic and strychnine, and daily massages. Vacation time and summertime being near, I followed his instructions, but refused to give up my studies entirely.

At this time Julia Sédova, a Russian ballerina, came to train with Clustine, and he having no studio of his own, asked the use of mine. It was with pleasure that I consented, for it was a stimulation to work with others. I was also recompensed, for Madame Sédova had a marvelous sense of criticism, of analyzing and grasping immediately what was needed for correction. Clustine was also interested in a dancer of the Paris opera, Marcel Bergé, saying that this young man was the most talented one in that organization. He came to work with us too. So we had a class of three regularly every morning. This enabled me to hear discussions of the dance from their respective points of view and so helped me in my own personal judgment. The Spectacles of Diaghilew beginning again, I saw other ballets and new creations. This was the "great epoch" of Diaghelew.

Adelaïde

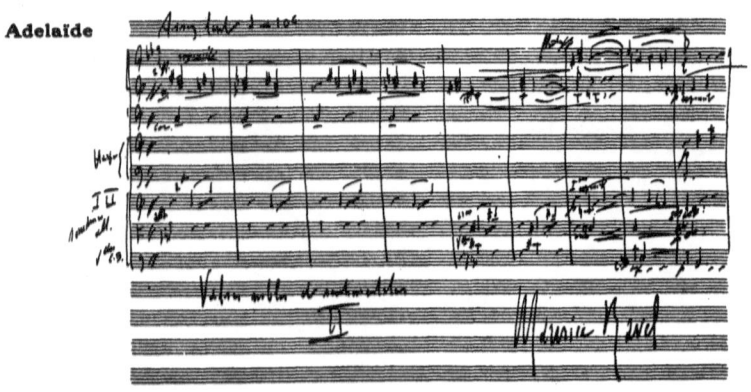

Salomé

Facsimile of musical script and signature of Maurice Ravel for the score of "Adelaide".
Also of Florent Schmitt for the score of "Salome".

OVERWORK

He created a new repertoire, rightly abandoning the old demoded ones of the Marinsky Theatre.

One ballet, remarkable among others of Michel Fokine, was the *Fire Bird,* with the wonderful music of Stravinsky and a fine personnel. This enthused me anew.

Tamara was also shown with a new setting by Leon Bakst. He created at this time one of the most beautiful works, *The St. Sebastian* of Gabriel d'Annunzio for Ida Rubenstein with her own organization, which in my opinion is the most beautiful of all spectacles in which I ever assisted.

Isadora Duncan also had a season at the Chatelet Theatre and I went to see her. At that period she was still more the dancer than the plastique tragedian. So I did not see her at her best, but later I again saw that genial woman and at that time recognized in her only the pioneer of a new movement rather than admired her as an executor of the dance. She had certainly made enormous progress in the dance, by realizing the possibilities of the "symphonic poem," interpreting them, instead of utilizing only the waltzes, gallops and polkas of the old school. She had the good taste to eliminate the old background of scenery and to replace it by the simplicity of a velvet curtain which set off the beauty of gesture and the plastique of the human body. She freed the feet of conventional foot-gear, toe slipper, ridiculous for the Greek, Oriental and other dances. Most estimable her innovation. But a foot a little bent can be beautiful on a bar-relief. In action, a foot, flat, is ugly. It is too primitive, too inartistic, too near the Zulu. The same type of costume is monotonous for all the dances and in the Greek dances her coiffure seemed to me also to be entirely lacking in style. At last, the summer vacation arrived just in time to interrupt the ardor of my studies. I obtained from my father permission to make a pleasure trip through Italy instead of returning to Russia.

There I did not completely abandon my exercises but took more time to rest with the aim of being in better condition to resume my work on my return to Paris.

OVERWORK

I visited Milan, Venice, Florence, Rome and Naples. I knew them well and it was always a joy to return to them, to see their incomparable treasures of art. I will not attempt to describe anything of these cities as a book could be written about each one of them. This would bring me too far from my subject. I returned to Paris at the end of the summer.

Pavlowa

I HAD never seen Pavlowa, as she had quitted the company of Diaghilew before I became interested in the "dance." She had formed a company of her own, had gone to London and then toured the United States of America. Now the Theatre des Champs Elysée announced a season of opera followed by divertissements and dances by Pavlowa. They talked much of Pavlowa, of her interpretations of *The Swan* by Saint Saëns. I was anxious to see her.

There were many little stories circulated about her, amusing anecdotes. I shall report a few of them though not vouching for their authenticity, having not been a witness. One was, that at a great gala event given by Diaghilew at the Opera in Paris, the banker, Otto Kahn, was in one of the loges intending to choose the best of the ballets' "teams," and present them to America. At this spectacle it had been decided to give a famous "pas de deux," always a great success, in which the virtuosity of the dancers was given full opportunity. Diaghilew had many stars in his organization. In this rivalry, two ballerinas contended. Diaghilew, himself, was greatly embarrassed because one of these two was Kschesinska, who was recognized as the ballerina of Russia. The other was Pavlowa, who had obtained the greatest success. She was now the favorite of Paris. I don't know which of these two dancers was announced on the program but neither one had given up the intention of doing that dance. Both were dressed, ready in the wings to appear en scene. Kschesinska, with her partner, Pavlowa with Mordkin as hers. The curtain lifted before the orchestra had started the music of the dance. Pavlowa, at this, quickly grasped the hand of Mordkin, led him after her and so took the center of the stage, and in doing so, she gained her point. To keep from creating a public scandal, Diaghilew had to let Pavlowa continue the dance. It was following this incident that, chosen by Otto Kahn to tour the United States, her great and glorious career began.

Another amusing narration about Pavlowa was as follows: She was introduced to London society at a great fête where she was carried in, in an enormous basket of flowers from which she had stepped to do her admirable dance, *The Swan*. Recognizing her great success, a society woman wanted to have her dance at one of her fêtes and so announced the fact before having made arrangements with Pavlowa as to the price she would ask. When she did receive Pavlowa's figure, she was amazed at the enormity of the sum and wrote her saying that she would pay the price as she had already announced her appearance at the fête, but she would not ask of Pavlowa in this case, that she remain among her guests after the execution of her dance. Pavlowa responded that she was absolutely satisfied with the arrangements but had she known in advance that she would not be expected to remain among the guests in the evening, she would have demanded a price less high. (I have heard lately a like story recounted of Kreisler in an American newspaper.)

The third anecdote they tell about Pavlowa is that she was very touchy, and that while playing at the Palace Theatre in London, a tiff occurred between Mordkin and her, and that after that they finished their season without ever speaking to one another and met only on the stage. These reports, augmented by the publicity given them by the press, gave the impression that Pavlowa was of a curious and unusual temperament in her private life as well as in her public one.

The season of opera at the Champs Elysée found the management in a very awkward position because of the difficulty of forming a repertoire. The Grand Opera de Paris as well as the Opera Comique, both subsidized by the government, possessed the exclusive rights to the principal operatic works, the old as well as the new. Because of this, they at the Champs Elysée were forced to fall back upon some old fashioned works; *Benvenuto Cellini* and *Lucia de Lammermoor* for one, the director, Astruck, resolved to produce these demoded works, but to give them a modern touch. Not to produce them in the spirit of the epoch of the libretto, but in the style of the first performance staged. So the *Lucia de Lammermoor* that I went to see was presented not in the atmosphere of the XVI century in accordance with its history, but as an amusing reproduction as created in the year 1855. This deviation was marvelously interpreted, but unfortunately this effort so artistic, refined and clever was appreciated by only a certain few and not by the general public. The marvelous singing of Marie Barrientos was absolutely incomparable and she was given a great ovation. Pavlowa followed this with her dancing. To dance following an opera is always an ungrateful condition for this reason: The audiences are evidently not particularly dance-minded and many times find the opera uninteresting. The public of Paris, used to the grande ballets of Diaghilew, were little interested in the divertissements of Pavlowa and many people left. I, coming with the intention of seeing her, felt that the applause accorded Barrientos left anything coming after less important.

The curtain lifted on a scene, banal and ordinary, which did not make Pavlowa stand out to any outstanding degree. Pavlowa appeared with her partner in the *Valse Caprice* of Rubenstein. It was the usual *pas de deux* of the old ballet. She danced it well, but her costume, Grecian, reminded me of a picture one sees on popular post cards. The dance that she presented had no particular interest but it gave her the opportunity to execute some pirouettes and to be carried off aloft by her partner as though she were a valuable piece of furniture. This conception of the old ballet of having the partner act as an elevator for the girls had always seemed to me ridiculous. However, Laurent Novikoff performed his task well.

The incomparable Anna Pavlowa in "Arebesque sur pointes" in her Swan costume. This picture is one of the most perfect dance poses ever to be taken by any dancer.

Pavlowa

Pavlowa accelerated and retarded the music at will with little musical understanding. I was absolutely disillusioned about her.

Following came her *Swan*. I preferred it to the *Valse Caprice*, and later seeing it from the wings, as time went on I liked its artistry and appreciated it more and more. I cannot say whether it was that Pavlowa was not in the mood or I was expecting too much or the atmosphere of the place was wrong, the unresponsiveness of the public, the triumph of Barrientos which would make the applause appear meagre accorded Pavlowa; whatever it was there was lack of contact between the public and the artist. Pavlowa had this peculiarity, she went from one extreme to another; she was never pretty, always either ugly or beautiful. Wearing a blonde wig, with her hair frizzed, she appeared to be of Semitic type but not of the better type. Coiffed with bandeau, à la Taglioni, or in a white wig, she showed a pure profile, delicate transparency, an exquisiteness, a distinction very aristocratic. She was ideal for the classic ballet. She was not the delicate and beautiful woman that Karsavina was, but the spirit of the dance incarnate. A sylph of transparent steel with ankles like a gazelle, not evoking her sex, but attracting exclusively the attention of the spectator by her art. The movements of her arms were marvelous, individual, different entirely from the conventional ones of the old ballet. The grace of her neck and her movements made me comprehend why they, the public, had so much admired her in *The Swan*, but I could not forgive her for wearing the common white tarlatane of the dancer, giving the frightful silhouette of a top, in an interpretation of the lover of Leda or the brother of Elsa.

Novikoff followed with a dance, the *Pirate*. He had very strong limbs and a face more tragic than pleasant. I should have liked to have seen him execute something more profound, more in accord with his facial expression, a rebellious angel—say, a composition unfolding a character more appropriate to his type than insipid jumping. After his number Pavlowa danced her *Butterfly*. Again she wore one of her horrible tarlatanes of a repulsive color. And had most banal music. But in spite of these facts, she appeared to me simply incomparable. She was indeed a true butterfly, fluttering, gathering (sweets), frisking, with such lightness and delicacy accomplishing a real choreographic stunt. She finished her program with her famous *Bacchanal* from the ballet of *Cléopatra*. Again my enthusiasm cooled. Her costume in cut and color again repelled me. Ida Rubenstein, in presenting *Helene of Sparta,* had divine attitudes, postures copied from Etruscan vases. She wore a peplum with draperies carrying archaic lines. Pavlowa, on the contrary, appeared in a costume of white with red dots; the effect was ugly. It was like a chemise or a dress for the summer made at some inexpensive dressmaking establishment. Instead of a work of picturesque gestures it was an avalanche, tiring, of interrupted movements, scintillating, recalling the cinema in its infancy. Her feet were neither nude nor in sandals; she wore something halfway, neither ballet or Greek, and being white, drew the attention unfortunately as a disadvantage to the feet; and worst of all, she wore tights that gave to the whole a look of cotton under-garments. It was bourgeois, Puritan, far from all that should be Greek. However, from these spectacles, I carried away with me the memory of a marvelous *Papillion*. But with that exception, the impression left upon me was far below that which I had after seeing the ballets of Diaghilew.

Impatience

I CONTINUED my study of the dance, working every morning under the tutelage of Clustine in company with Julia Sédova and with Marcel Bergé, but I was beginning to become impatient and ardently desired that Clustine would at last give his consent to my appearing in public.

Ida Rubenstein, making alteration in her studio, continued her training under Clustine in mine, which I had put at her disposal, but she came only in the afternoons. She was preparing for the grand spectacles for the springtime. One was the *Pizanelle* of Gabriel D'Annunzio, a dramatic poem in which she appeared in the double role of tragedienne and danseuse.

This environment of theatrical activity made me resent more and more my own inactivity.

After having refused many times to appear in social functions, due to Clustine always saying that I was not yet ready, I at last won his consent to dance at a great charitable event given under the supervision of Madame Tassard, President of the Society of Women Musicians of France. In it were to appear celebrated performers and as an attraction new and exceptional Clustine permitted me to appear; my first appearance in public as a dancer. I cannot express the importance of this to me—how nervous and excited I was after such long anticipation.

Clustine rehearsed me in my steps, but I, myself, originated a

Impatience

musical sketch representing the biblical serpent tempting Eve with the forbidden fruit.

My appearance was sensational, the public saying that a dancer comparable to Nijinsky had appeared.

After this great success Clustine permitted me to repeat this dance at another event and I received the same eulogies; but if the first spectacle, because of its newness, enthused me, the second disillusioned me, for it was also for charity and not a real professional engagement. My third appearance was in an Oriental dance presented at the Theatre Fémina aux Champs Elysées in a play written by a friend. In this event, which was not a charity performance, I had the occasion to have the comments of the press, which were excellent for me, and a very smart audience for the premiere because of the social relations of my father.

But I still was dissatisfied as, according to my opinion, I had not made my real debut. For the third time I had performed without pay. It was not so much a question of gain as it would have been satisfaction to know that my work had received some remuneration to prove to myself a recognition. So, these appearances at long intervals instead of encouraging me had just the opposite effect, and I began to ask myself if all my efforts, all my hard work, were in vain, if I was following a simple Chimera.

I had an offer from an impressario to whom Clustine had presented me, for the position of premiere danseur at the Opera of Vienna, but the remuneration was small and Clustine would not allow me to accept it, so I was at a loss as to what to do. A position in the Grand Opera or in the Opera Comique of Paris was hardly possible. These establishments, subsidized by the French government, employed only artists of their own country or outsiders having a certain renown, but not someone like myself without, truth to say, any real theatrical experience.

The music halls of Paris employed little of high class attractions and if a ballet was presented they preferred a feminine soloist, often the question was one less of talent than dishabille.

Impatience

Diaghilew was so occupied with Nijinsky that he would not dream of taking with him a dancer who could expect to approach him. The ballerinas were all marvelous but there was no chance for the individual male dancer on account of Nijinsky (except in parts grotesque and character). Nothing must take from the glory of the star, and to Nijinsky was reserved the exclusive right of originality and exoticism. Michel Fokine, already established and grand master in his organization, decided to abandon it. All horizons to me seemed closed and a melancholic disappointment seemed the fruit of all efforts.

Serge Oukrainsky in the "Minuete" by Mozart.

Monsieur Dandré

As a conversation at the table changed my mode of life, an unexpected visit influenced my entire destiny. Without any notification Clustine brought to my studio a gentleman demanding that Marcel Bergé and I dance for him. He introduced this gentleman, Monsieur Dandré, as the personal manager of the already celebrated Anna Pavlowa, and who was reorganizing a troupe to make a two-year tour of the world. He had met Clustine at the Opera and had asked him if he could recommend any dancers, and Clustine had diplomatically told him that he had two pupils he was training and that if he had time he would like him to come and visit the class and see what they were doing.

When we had finished our dance Monsieur Dandré was most enthusiastic, the moreso probably as he had expected to meet only two students in which he might see only possibilities. He said that if it depended upon him alone he would engage us then, but being only the manager of Madame Pavlowa he could not do it without her personal approbation. She, he said, was in London at that time, dancing at the Palace Theatre, but to overcome this inconvenience, he would take it upon himself, if we were at liberty, to invite us and pay for our transportation and for our sojourn in London so that she could personally see and be judge of our talents. We accepted this proposition with great joy and it was decided that the following week we would depart for London.

The celebrated Dutch dancer, Andreas Pavley.

Ivy House

Though I had travelled much and London was so near to Paris, I had never been to England.

Monsieur Dandré very courteously made reservations for us in a boarding house which catered to artists and dancers. There I made the acquaintance of Constantin Kobeleff, who danced with Pavlowa; of Madame Estaphiewa, who was with Diaghilew; of the partner of Lydia Kyasht and others.

The day after our arrival we went to Ivy House, the residence of Anna Pavlowa. She received us graciously with the greatest simplicity, a characteristic always of a great artist or of a woman of the best world. I have always noticed that the mediocre or the upstarts are the ones of most pretention.

She offered us a cup of tea served *à la Russe* from a samovar of silver, then showed us her house, her studio encumbered with baskets full of costumes ready for use, and loads of flowers, homages laid at her feet. She showed us her garden with its lovely pond at the side of which she interpreted her famous *Swan*.

I was particularly interested to make the acquaintance of Andreas Pavley, whom I found most distinguished, with an allure and a manner which set him apart advantageously from the rest of the entourage.

The one who intrigued me the most was the famous Cecchetti, the celebrated master of the ballet, the *doyen* and arbitar par excellence in choreographic questions. Pavlowa had him as instructor

Serge Oukrainsky in his celebrated Persian Dance.

to direct her and her company and also act as mime. For the more modern dances and novelties she had another ballet master of great talent, a Pole, "Monsieur Zaylich," who was also the premier character dancer.

Pavlowa gave us tickets for evening performance at the Palace Theatre and also made an appointment with us for the morrow after the matinee. We were to dance for her then.

Her performance at the Palace was very much the same as I had seen her give at the Champs Elysée in Paris. *The Valse Caprice, The Swan, The Bacchanal, A Butterfly on a Rose* danced by Constantin Kobeloff and premier classic dancer, Mademoiselle Plaskowieczka, a pretty Warsobien. *A Moment Musicale* executed by three danseuses. *Second Rhapsody* of Liszt, led by the premier character dancer Mademoiselle Gachewska, another very beautiful Polaniese and Monsieur Zaylich, the master of the ballet. The premier classic dancer was Novikoff, Pavlowa's partner in the numbers of this style.

The performance was very good; the company was excellent but I found nothing extraordinary; nothing new or original. As to Pavlowa, I appreciated her more seeing her dance this second time.

The next day, the day for our audition, I met Pavlowa coming from the stage and she gave an order for a dressing room in which to change.

Marcel Bergé executed a classic variation.

I danced a *Persian Dance* on which I had worked under Clustine. Part of the emotion which I felt was due to the importance this would be to me in securing an engagement, but even more it was due to the knowledge that I was to be judged by Pavlowa, who was recognized as one of the principal authorities on these matters, and added to this was the fact that I was dancing on the stage of the Palace Theatre, the first time that I had been on a stage so constructed with a very deep slope.

Pavlowa complimented us profusely. This showed how sincere she and Monsieur Dandré were, for it was not to their interest to show too great enthusiasm for fear we would demand too high a salary. If they had been like some of the hardened managers I came to know later they would scarcely have expressed approbation, but, true artists as they were, they gave us great praise. Monsieur Zaylich, particularly, was most pleased. He planned to stage an entirely new oriental ballet and saw in me an exceptional discovery and explained that he meant to have a character especially created in his ballet so that I could introduce my *Persian Dance*.

Bergé and I were enchanted.

The conditions and terms of the contract were discussed with Monsieur Dandré. Anna Pavlowa had to do only with the artistic side of the matter, leaving the business arrangements to him.

We came to a satisfactory agreement regarding money matters. There were three clauses which I asked to be inserted in my contract. The first, that I was engaged principally for my specialties— dancing the *genre nouveau* and not the routine of the old ballet. The second clause, more difficult to obtain, was to have the contract for but a year. I feared to engage for a longer time. Two years then seemed so long. This was also agreed upon, but proved later to be a very unnecessary clause. The third was that, due to the fact that there were only thirty-five dancers in the company, I would from time to time, have to appear in dances not of my repertoire, but not in any Russian character dances. Clustine had commanded me to be strict on this point, for the bends executed in these dances are fatal to the limbs of a classic dancer; they cause the knees to become gross and crooked; the calves knotted and so deforming the lines of the legs by producing short, knotted muscles instead of the long, harmonious ones which make the beauty of the limbs. Having come to accord on all these points, we signed our contracts and departed for Paris to announce the good news to Clustine.

He was delighted, feeling that his years of instruction were to reap their reward. We went to work with renewed enthusiasm, but we had some months to wait, for Pavlowa was not to begin the tour until the Autumn and it was not yet Spring.

Serge Oukrainsky

THE ONE most astonished at this engagement was my father. He never imagined that I had taken it so seriously, never realized the hard work and all the effort I had expended on it. So, this engagement as soloist with Pavlowa who, even at this time, was recognized as one of the premiere dancers of the world, was a great surprise to him. Above all, that I had won it on my merits without any influence or pecuniary help. He was both proud and disgruntled; proud to know that his son had such talent and vexed to think of my using it professionally.

He had given his consent in the first place, thinking it only a caprice on my part, and approved of my appearing at social and charitable functions, but now my being a professional froze him, worried him, by the idea of "what will they say," pretending that my family could object to seeing the name on theatrical programs would demand that I take a stage name. Nothing could have pleased more. I wanted my success to be based on just my own self and my own efforts.

I took the name of *Serge,* never liking the one my parents had given me. This was simple for me to decide, but choosing a pseudonym was not so easy. All those that came to my mind seemed too banal or too pretentious, without any *raison d'etre.* Suddenly the idea came to me to take the name of the country in which I was born. Ukraine had a certain harmonious sound to me and my being born in Odessa gave it a raison d'etre. So prefixing an "O" to have the right pronunciation, I made the name Oukrainsky and thus was born in 1913 the dancer Serge Oukrainsky.

Before departing for London, Clustine had Bergé and me arrange some special numbers to add to those of Pavlowa's divertissements. He arranged for her *un pas de trois Greque* to the music of Goddard, in which she represented a *Bacchante*, Bergé *un Ephebe*, and I, *un faun*, kidnapping the disciple of Dyonisius. Another number represented a serpent and a bird, danced to the music of Mendelssohn. Clustine wished me to have also a Gavotte to dance with Pavlowa and for it he employed the popular music of the *Glow Worm*. I found the choice of this music deplorable and showed my lack of interest in it, not foreseeing the imminent success that it proved to be. Clustine conferred to Bergé its execution, but I had my Persian dance with the music of Moursorgsky and these creatings were the numbers which later became our leads.

For these dances Pavlowa had me design the costumes, knowing that I had studied painting, which I was very pleased to do without charge and was most happy to see fulfilled the conceptions of my ideas.

Second and True Debut

BERGÉ and I arrived in London ready to commence our rehearsals with Pavlowa. We lived in the same boarding house in which we had stayed on our first visit and we rehearsed in a big hall that Pavlowa had rented for this purpose, her own atelier being too small, she not having the use of the stage of the Palace Theatre exclusively for herself.

I was surprised to learn that almost all the young women dancers were her pupils, young English girls disguised more or less under Russian names. The men were, for the most part, Poles and were very good character dancers.

The principal artists were the celebrated Enrico Cecchetti, master of the ballet and instructor; Monsieur Zaylich, master of the ballet for the new repertoire; Laurent Novikoff, as classic partner; I for my part in *Nouveau genre*; and Bergé and Kobeleff as premier danseurs; Mademoiselle Plaskowieczka, premier classic danseuse; and Mademoiselle Gachewska, premier character danseuse.

The ballet exotique, arranged by Zaylich, was in the "genre de *Tamara*," and pleased me infinitely, not only because I danced the part of the favorite slave, the principal male figure of the ballet, but also because the settings and the costumes were designed by Léon Bakst, the music well chosen despite the fact that it was a pot pourri, but the ensemble very artistic. They had entitled this ballet *Oriental Fantasies*.

One could not say the same of the *Magic Flute* of Drigo, which

Second and True Debut

Cecchetti placed after the choreography of Petipa. It was an old ballet set to the most banal of music and the whole arrangement was demoded in the extreme. Not yet being familiar with the repertoire and the taste of Pavlowa, I was amazed that a ballet like this would be made a part of her program, expecting, rather, that she would present the ballets especially written for her or dances interpreting symphonic poems.

Misfortune came to me at one of the rehearsals; I sprained my ankle. My anguish was great, not alone from the pain of the foot, but for fear that I would lose my engagement and not be able to continue my work.

I returned to the house desolate but decided to do all possible to combat my bad luck. Knowing that my foot was not broken, as I could manage to walk on it, I did not consult a doctor, but did what I thought best myself. After bathing it in warm salted water and the juice of a lemon, I applied a compress of embrocation. The warmth eased the pain and arrested the inflammation. I felt much better and slept happily, feeling that it would be all right.

But on awakening in the morning I was stupefied to see that the sprain was not all of the trouble—there had formed a blister and the skin came off with the bandage causing me to suffer agonies. I nearly fainted not only from the pain but from the thought not to be able to rehearse and lose the engagement. At last with a Spartasiette stoism I managed with agony to put a sock on top of the bandage and, cutting a shoe, I managed to go limping to the rehearsal. Even for an old trouper it is difficult to learn a dance without having executed it, but for me, a beginner, to learn from memory only was a veritable *tour de force*. When I had to learn steps I could mark them with the hands, but when I have to change places on the stage I was forced to hop on one foot across the floor.

Fortunately, the two masters of the ballet were very indulgent and saw how hard I worked to overcome my handicap.

After about a month of rehearsing, Pavlowa gave two farewell performances in London at the London Opera House, "the place of

Second and True Debut

my real debut". My wound was not yet healed and it was not until we arrived in America that the skin had completely formed, but the scar remained for a number of years.

The Spectacle in London was for me a new emotion—appearing before the public as a real professional engagement and more than that, with the knowledge that Diaghilew was in the audience, and many other celebrities, also the London Press. The criticisms of my work were excellent in spite of the fact that I was not at my best, each step causing agony. I was happy to continue and not to have lost my engagement.

Anna Pavlowa in the "Dragon Fly".

Crossing the Ocean

PAVLOWA LOVED everything German and she chose the steamer Kaiser Wilhelm II to bring us to the United States. She travelled first-class and the company second; my transportation was furnished to me in the same way. I could have paid the difference, having always traveled first class, but thought it better taste to do as the others did—I desired to get on a friendly footing with the members of the company and did not want to be thought a snob.

I had made many crossings from Constantinople to Trieste, passing marvelous islands like Corfu and admiring the coast lines of the countries softened by the maritime mists, so I found the crossing of the Atlantic very monotonous and lacking in interest.

With the troupe as a whole I found that I had very little in common. Instead of calling Anna Pavlowa by her name or calling her Madame Pavlowa, or simply Pavlowa, as celebrities are usually spoken of, they referred to her as *Madame,* which gave the effect of subalterns or even of servants. It was only Monsieur Dandré, Pavley and I who used the other address.

They formed into little cliques—Cecchetti with a pupil, a protege of his, and two Italians; Zaylich had with him the two Polish premiere dancers and the group of Polish dancers; the little English girls kept to themselves; Novikoff with his wife; my group was the most cosmopolitan. It was the most intellectual, made up of a young Englishman named Marini, who had *"de l'esprit";* of Kobeleff, a Russian, who was a comrade of the school of Pavlowa; of Pavley, who was

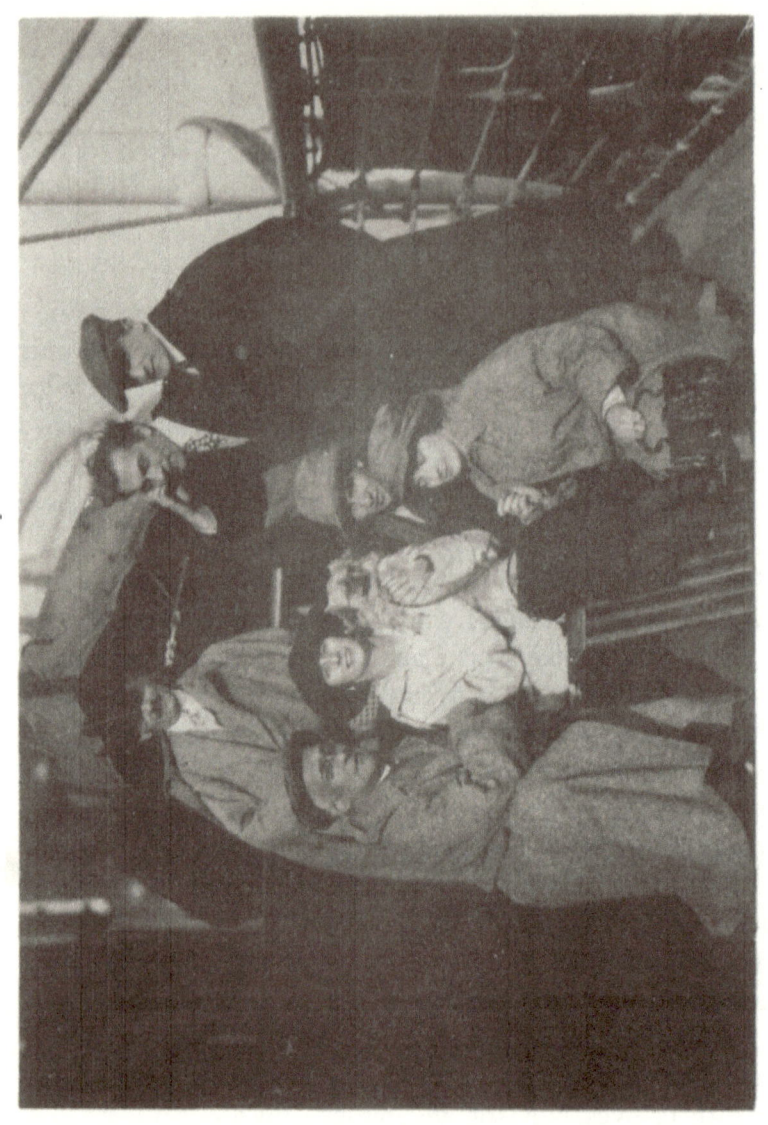

Snapshot of S. S. Kaiser Wilhelm—left to right: Maestro Cecchetti; Theodore Stier (musical director); Anna Pavlowa; Andreas Pavley, a student of Cecchetti; Serge Oukrainsky and Constantine Kobeleff.

very intellectual; he was Dutch. He came, as I, from a very good family, but all with the exception of his mother disapproved of his choice of a career. He had been a pupil of Jacques Delcrose and, though still very young, had had a company in England and accomplished a great success, but being of fine mind and ambitious, he realized the necessity of more study to perfect himself, so, having difficulties with his partner, he had accepted this engagement with the special aim of perfecting himself under the counsel of Cecchetti and of Pavlowa.

These groups formed on shipboard continued on land, with the exception that we often joined the company of Pavlowa and Monsieur Dandré.

Having been a frequenter of artistic sets in Paris, I had often remarked of the kinship of the different arts; a conversation often started on one topic of the arts ended by talking about one of the sister arts. I was surprised to find that, with the exception of Pavlowa and our group, the company were not artists, but only dancers. I was expecting more personality. The English girls had the mentality of other little English girls; they were too young and were like boarding school groups. The Pole element, with the exception of Zaylich, were not highly educated, and I really did not have anything in common with them. With them it was less an art than a business; just technical subjects discussed with the attitude of artisans, where to get the best food reasonably priced, their engagements and their salaries.

As our boat approached New York, the outline of the city against the horizon seemed most familiar, made so to me by the American films that I had seen. A certain beauty, a grandeur as of human power, as some towers of Babel reaching to the skies instead of Psalms rising from the spire of Goethic Cathedrals; this was the picture of money piled on top of money, on a stair-like effect of the skyscraper. A lack of harmony in the composition made one feel as if it was all done only to flatter the almighty dollar. This inequality in height gave the sensation as of a city constructed on a hill. It gave the impression to arrive in a town like Naples, but less picturesque, cold, but with great power.

The formalities of landing, with all the red tape which spoils the pleasure of most travel, had to be gone through with. I always resented going back to Russia—the verification of passports and so forth. Traveling on the continent, the custom official simply demands, "Have you anything to declare?" They acquit themselves quickly, happy to have it over with, fearful of having been a bother. On the Russian frontier it was not the same; they give the impression of a state case. But in America, the most modern of countries, the situation would still be worse. In Europe one travels as a tourist, as a visitor, or as in the case of being one of a theatrical company. In the United States one is considered as an emigrant and is visited by the doctor and the immigration officials. For some reason Kobeleff and I, having displeased one of them, he refused to allow us to land. Great men are always broadminded and have intelligence, but the small nature like to give themselves much importance and to give orders, doing acts of authority. I suppose to themselves they are somebody. Stupidity is the curse of the world. All debarqued but we two and we were kept on the boat for the night, the next day to be sent to Ellis Island to have it decided whether or not we were eligible and worthy to enter the United States. Max Rabinoff, Pavlowa's tour manager, came aboard to see what caused our delay. He could not understand what caused our being kept from landing unless it was that some overly zealous official was trying to show his authority. Learning that I had no money, having spent all that I had on replenishing my wardrobe, he advanced me some from my salary. One must have fifty dollars to enter the United States. The next day we debarqued to Ellis Island and were thrown among all types of emigrants, and had to stay there until late in the afternoon. They made us pass from hall to hall, but not understanding English, I did not know what they were saying. I had traveled in Turkey not speaking Turkish, in Italy ignorant of Italian, in Germany without knowing that language, but always I found someone who could interpret for me in Russian or in French. In America it seemed as if there was only the one language, English, and that all others appertained to another planet.

We were kept in a room with barred windows and a grilled door. Being behind bars was a novel experience for me and it amused me; and to look through the barricaded window and see the Statue of Liberty overlooking the port of New York seemed to me a bit ironic, paradoxical.

We at last learned that they had marked on our cards *"nervous"*, and they were to put us through an examination to deny this fact. The tests were so simple, like child's play, that one would be a complete idiot if not able to pass. We had to stand on one foot to see if we could keep our balance; that, too, was amusing, as it is one of my specialties. The second test seemed to me even more ridiculous. I am sure I could stand on one leg longer than this officer could stand on both his feet after taking a pint of whiskey. At last I could guess that the inspector who had been making our examination could not understand himself why they had made our landing difficult. He seemed to be more kind, occupying a higher position than the other man. I could have been in a bad mood if the absurdity of such procedures had not amused me greatly. So our visas were signed, permitting us to enter America. Rabinoff conducted us to the hotel York on Seventh Avenue, where most of the company had registered.

Exact reproduction of the famous Pavlowa Gavotte
statue, posed by Anna Pavlowa for
Malvina Hoffman.

New York

New York pleased me only by the fact that it was a great metropolis. It had not the beauty of the capitals of Europe, but an irregularity of outline. A shack-like place next to a large building in the middle of the town shocked my esthetic nature and I have not found a single place whose architecture could compare with the Place Vendome or Place de la Concorde.

We were to appear at the Metropolitan, but to break-in our performance we went first to a small town not far from New York. This was new to me; instead of having a dress rehearsal and then a general for the elite, they gave for an economical reason this performance, trying it out on the public who paid the price, thinking they were seeing a perfected performance. The town so sacrificed was Meriden.

Pavlowa danced for the first time the *Pavlowa Gavotte,* which later became famous; Bergé was her partner. I was disillusioned with the costume which I had designed and then saw for the first time. The chapeau worn by Pavlowa, instead of being like those of the "*Merveilleuses*" of the Directoir period, was more like those of the time of Dickens. The train of her costume was too short and could not be thrown nonchalantly over the arm but had to be tacked to a ribbon attached to her wrist. In the most illogical manner Mr. Dandré, who made no objection to the ballet skirt which showed the leg to the hip, objected to the slit on the side of the skirt *(it being of Récamier period)* and demanded that lace be added; it jutted out making a very ugly line, giving the effect of an old-fashioned petticoat. Bergé preferred not to wear the bicorne, which gave the effect of a personage of the "*Incroyables*". But despite these incorrect details, the effect was as a whole attractive and my creations were copied many times.

The Gavotte established itself as a great success and became one of the regular specialties. Pavlowa was raised to the seventh heaven of delight not only from the fact that she had a new sensational number but one that didn't call for dancing on the toes and so saved her that strain.

I was happy to quit Meriden. I like the large cities or the seaside or the country, but abhor the spirit of the provincial towns. I had been thinking that a great artist like Pavlowa would visit only the principal cities of the country like Diaghilew had been doing; it was another surprise for me to know that there was not a single one-horse town that was not on her itinerary. The only consolation that I had was to learn that we had to stay there but a day.

Returning to New York and having some time to spare I decided to look around and see the city, and rejoin the company later at the theatre. Getting on Broadway finally I tried as best I could to ask an officer to direct me to the Metropolitan Opera House, but he treated me with scorn; it was not like London where they were most courteous. I decided to ask someone more obliging—the passerby—but supposing that I did not understand well I passed and repassed many times between Thirty-fifth and Forty-second streets in quest of the famous Metropolitan. I was searching for a sumptuous edifice like the Grand Opera of Paris or the Bourg Theatre in Vienna, or the Opera of Odessa, one worthy of the city of New York.

At last my eye was attracted by a sign announcing the Pavlowa Spectacle so I thought that I would ask there to be directed to the theatre and they told me that this was the Metropolitan Opera House and I, not understanding English well, believed I had been directed to the Store House of the Opera House. I could not have imagined that this old building was the famous Metropolitan. I decided to find some of the stage crew working there and ask them to direct me to it. What a surprise to find that I was there on the stage. The interior was more acceptable, although it had no grand marble stairs, no paintings of the masters in the foyer; in fact none of the luxury one ascribes to a Grand Opera House. Only upon seeing the rest of the company there was I convinced that it was the theatre in which we were to play. I have found lately in America that the railroad stations look like theatres, but the theatres usually have a deplorable aspect. Their greatness also is not judged in accord to the size of the stage, in consideration of the possibility to produce magnificent performances, but according to the number of seats allowing to expect big box-office returns.

We gave a season at the Metropolitan before going on tour. Pavlowa had been here once before with Mordkin, but this was the first time with her own company. The program consisted of the horrible *Magic Flute* by Drigo, of the *Oriental Fantasy,* and of the divertissements.

I received enormous applause for my *Persian Dance* which Zaylich had introduced in the *Oriental Ballet* for me. At the end of the act, Pavlowa came before the curtain to acknowledge the great reception, she returned again taking Novikoff, who was her partner, with her, and then she turned towards me to have me salute the public with her. The applause redoubled itself, a veritable ovation. I was very happy and very confused for I had heard that she was selfish and jealous as to the applause. Pavlowa followed this number with her *Gavotte* and reaped a great triumph, winning new laurels. After the *Oriental Ballet* I had lingered on the stage in the wings near Daniel Mayer (he was Pavlowa's English manager) and Monsieur Dandré. I heard Mayer say to Dandré, "It is not good for Madame Pavlowa," and then seeing me said to Dandré, "Come I wish to talk more with you," and they went farther off.

New York

The next day Monsieur Dandré explained to me in a very diplomatic way, but with some embarrassment, about the change they wanted to make in my dance. He pretended that Monsieur Zaylich, the master of the ballet who had arranged all these dances for the *Oriental Fantasy,* desired that I would not use in his ballet a dance arranged by another ballet master; he would modify and rearrange my dance so it would be as of his composition. I was greatly surprised, since my engagement had been due to the desire of Monsieur Zaylich to introduce this dance into his work. I realized immediately that I was face to face with the tactique mostly American, "the one-star system." So I was faced with either one or two solutions: to break and leave the company or to accept this explanation and go on. I felt glad that I had not signed for more than a year if this was the treatment Pavlowa accorded her dancers. It seemed to me that it being her own organization the success of any one of the company would indirectly reflect on her.

I came to the conclusion that I had best remain the year and have more or less success and then would find it easier to get another engagement. By breaking now they would probably say that my work was unsatisfactory. So I reflected that it was best for me to give the impression that I believed this pretext and so I responded that I understood very well the scrupulous sentiment of Monsieur Zaylich and that I would be happy to have a dance arranged in accord with the choreographic of the ballet made by him.

Zaylich rearranged the music and the dance. I made a success of it, even changed as it was, but nothing to compare with my other interpretation which made me a rival of Pavlowa. This arrangement seemingly satisfied everybody.

General Happenings

During our stay in New York we rehearsed at Bryant Hall. It was not as brilliant as the name suggested. It is a place where, with antiquated pianos, theatrical companies rehearse all sorts of stunts amid discarded cigar stumps, cigarette ashes and dried gum sticking to the chairs and boards. It seemed strange to me that Pavlowa could not find a better studio for rehearsals, being compelled to use such a place.

Before rehearsals Cecchetti always gave a class lesson. The young girls were assiduous in their attendance but Novikoff rarely came, pretending to suffer a heart ailment and did not want to overwork himself. The men of the company, perhaps because of laziness or for lack of ambition, did not attend regularly as did Kobeleff, Pavley and myself.

The school of Cecchetti differed slightly from that of Clustine. The steps were more complicated and smaller, but Clustine's school required more endurance, as everything was broader and with more elevation.

There were no dressing rooms in this hall and screens were put up, one side for the girls and in another corner for the men. Being only three or four of us to change, and as the English girls were of a large number, they appropriated our corner besides their own space; as a result we could not change in order to take the class and had to miss them, and for the rehearsals we had to use our street clothes and spoil them by taking poses on the floor, then keep

Costume sketch designed by Serge Oukrainsky
for Anna Pavlowa for the
Pavlowa Gavotte.

our linen on after it was soiled with perspiration. The first time that this happened I objected to their behavior and asked them politely to stay in their own quarters. The next day it again happened; and they had paid no attention to my request. I asked them again, telling them how inconvenient it was to rehearse in civilian clothes and that I did not intend to stop my choreographic study because of their lack of consideration. The third day it happened the same way and they laughed at my discontent. I told them this would be the last time they would act in such a manner and if they continued I would teach them a lesson to stay in their own place.

I always thought it was the proper manner to act a gentleman in regard to women, to help them and to be courteous, but on the other hand I think it most absurd and provincial to let them sit on your head and allow them everything and to take advantage under pretext of their sex.

The fourth day I came for the lesson and rehearsal the same thing existed. "Alright, I told you this corner is reserved for the men to change; you may stay if you wish, but I will not take any consideration of your presence. This will not handicap me to change my clothes for the exercises. You certainly will not be the first girls I have seen in the nude, having lived in Paris and frequented art studios. A few more or less is immaterial to me. I have also been in the *Bal des Quat-Z-Arts* where I, myself, was practically nude among three thousand people in the same brief attire, so a dozen girls won't bother me." Telling them this, I stepped behind the screen and started quietly to undress in the middle of a lot of shouting. All upset, the girls dressed as fast as they could and rushed from behind the screen in a great fury. It was now my turn to laugh at them, and I considered they had gotten what they deserved.

This caused a regular revolution in the ballet and the girls complained to Pavlowa of what I had done. She called me to reprimand me, but was unable to keep a straight face, not attaching any seriousness to the incident because I did it only to gain my point and to be able to continue with the lessons. She told me, however, that my actions could cause her unpleasantness, since it could be interpreted in an evil manner and she would appreciate it if I would apologize to the girls.

I was furious with the girls and my intention was to shock them in order to punish them for their selfishness and for their lack of consideration. I realized that Pavlowa was right; in the meantime I did not want to have given the impression that I was not in the right. I said to one of the girls that represented their group, "Madame Pavlowa asked me to make my excuse to you but I feel that I was within my right and will do the same thing again if necessary, but to please Madame Pavlowa I will ask you to excuse me." They accepted this kind of apology and we became very good friends and had no more trouble.

Before leaving Europe I had purchased a guide book of Bedecker with the intention of seeing in my spare time the American cities and what would be of interest to visit. I was very disappointed in what there was to see. Europe has too much of the cult of the ancient and the respect of the past. America, on the contrary, abhors it. America is really the country of the present, having in view the future without any sentiment of the past. The modern comfort is greatly superior to the European one. What is a luxury there, is, in America, a simple necessity and the convenience can be found at less expense. But you cannot find in America the great luxury of Europe. America will always be a new country because nothing is built with the idea to stay, but always temporarily with the idea to be destroyed as soon as they can perfect something better. The museums, with the exception of some great masters, have little to show except of reproduction of Chefs d'oeuvres of which I have seen the original. I was not expecting to find a great deal of antiquity, but anyway little vestiges of the past. Much later when I visited Mexico, which is not a country older than the United States, I found much more historical remembrances.

Besides the natural curiosities like the Grand Canyon, Yellowstone Park and Niagara Falls, I could not find human artistic creations. The falls of Niagara, which are really grandios, disappointed me, anyway, by lack of proportion; they are much too large in rapport of their height. The nature there has a lack of composition. Traveling from town to town, I was surprised by their likeness. Their sizes vary, but the aspect is the same: one main street, a few five and ten cent stores, two or three large hotels and the practical monotony, but with lack of picturesqueness, blocks of houses divided in checker form. The absence of trees on the avenues and streets added to the general coldness of the picture. New York is the model after which follows smaller editions; Chicago, Philadelphia and after all, the other towns. The only ones which make exceptions of this rule are Boston, which resembles an English town; Washington, which has the aspect of some German cities; New Orleans with its fanformed streets, keeps the aspect of a French colony, and San Francisco and Los Angeles, which possess the advantage of a picturesque nature, remind one of the towns on the coast of the Riviera. What surprised me most was to find so few statues in the parks. I was reared in the view of the *Garden of Versailles,* of the Louvre, of the Tuilleries, of the Place de Concorde. Traveling, I have visited *Shoenbrun* near Vienna, *La Villa Medecias* of Rome.

But I found nothing of this kind of beauty in America. Complete lack of statues, and if by exception I found one it was always of a political man, a president or a pioneer. I have a great reverence for Abraham Lincoln, a great man, humanitarian, with a beautiful soul; I believe they should perpetuate his memory in a country for which he did so many fine and beautiful things, and it is quite natural to place his statue in many places. But a Puritan *redingote,* even if it was philanthropic, lacked the esthetic and if they accord some homage to it this should offer no cause for not exhibiting beautiful sculpture, a handsome body of man or a graceful figure of woman in order to decorate the square or the gardens in honor of the beautiful, in contrast to the comic pages of the American newspapers which establish in the mind the taste for the grotesque and the comic.

Andreas Pavley in a perfect plain Arabesque.

[78]

General Happenings

On the contrary, and from the industrial point of view, there are many interesting things to visit in America. The stockyards in Chicago is a celebrated place, but I did not go to see it, afraid that it might discourage my taste for meat. I am not a vegetarian by taste and the physical efforts required by my art prohibits me to become one. I have visited the Ford Automobile factory, and found it really extraordinary on point of view of order, cleanliness and the way of management of the organization. Leaving, I had a feeling of depression as I saw man reduced to a state of machinery. If a working man works on some mechanism he can make a new discovery, experimenting to find a new invention, but there the system does not allow one to do so. Each man must always do the same piece of work, doing it the same way with a limited amount of time, like being in a nightmare; also, like a nightmare, a new piece arrives in front of him always before he has time to finish the previous one in order to push him to work faster; such sameness and such tension without need of imagination would be enough to drive one mad, I felt.

I soon had to discard in a corner of my trunk my Bedecker, not having good use for it. The tour as a whole was monotonous, always the same, with the exception of some incidents which I will describe later.

Andreas Pavley practicing under the direction of Cecchetti in a plain attitude position.

Pavlowa Intime

In New York, before going on tour, Pavlowa and I had engaged in a light flirtation and one day, being alone with her, I had taken her in my arms to embrace her. "*You Parisien,*" she said, "you truly are unafraid." Our tête-a-tête was interrupted before I had time to make a response. The next day, in talking to me, she took an attitude maternal, which the difference in our ages hardly permitted but as directress of the tour did allow. She scolded me gently for my audacity. In America, a boy having a love affair with a woman is considered a bad subject and is cause for real scandal. In France, a boy who has passed the age of sixteen has the advice of the family doctor to take care of his puberty. He is mocked and teased by his comrades in school if he has not a mistress; they consider him like an eunuch or a sexless person.

To have a liaison with Pavlowa at that time would have flattered my vanity, but I really was not in love with her. I had acted under an impulse and quickly regretted it, realizing that it could not have had a happy denouement, for even at that time Monsieur Dandré was in love with her and later married her. This would have created very unnecessary complications.

I was glad that she took this attitude with me. I excused myself by saying that my admiration for her as a great artist had carried me beyond myself and that it would never happen again. She looked as though she was half satisfied and half melancholic; we never talked again about this incident and the equivalent never happened.

Pavlowa Intime

It is difficult to describe Pavlowa, for she was made up of many contrasts. Her education at the Imperial school must have been very rudimentary, but she was very shrewd and very adaptable. Having known many people and those of the highest rank, she was always at ease, a great artist and a wordly woman, also much of a child in her professional jealousy. This trait of hers became legendary not as a sentiment of a mean nature but as a childish one. She seemed to take a delight in this attitude.

She was very strict with the members of her company, insisting upon punctuality. Later, having a company of my own, I realized how necessary this was.

As a dancer Pavlowa was truly admirable and incomparable. It was not that as a technician she could execute all the steps impeccably, dancing so is not sometimes more than acrobatics. The "fouetés," for example, I have seen done better by other dancers. Her specialty was doing certain steps in a fashion unsurpassable and, above all, personal. She had broken away from the old ballet postures of the arms and introduced the beauty of the Hellenic. All her movements were harmonious. She had the great art of making the effect simple but conveying the thought; no unnecessary gesture. Her slim body, nervous like that of a deer, seconded marvelously the style she had adopted.

I made a special study of the way she used her arms. In her taste and choice of a repertoire she followed the traditional tendency, but in the use of the arms she was absolutely revolutionary. She very much admired Isadora Duncan, knowing that there could be no rivalry of comparison between them.

Unfortunately, in spite of her adoration for the dance, she would do little to educate the ignorant to its true beauty; on the contrary, she played up to the taste of the general public and would present that which was banal and old if it would please them in order that she would stand out. Musically, also, to obtain an effect she would not hesitate to change the composition of the composers for her personal needs, changing the time to suit herself, making the cuts and repeats more or less good. If the director of the orchestra protested she responded, "They do not come to hear the music, they come to see Pavlowa dance." She was proud of her success and did not believe any contemporary dancer compared to her. Ignoring Karsavina and Kschesinska, I heard her say many times, "They speak now of Taglioni; the generations of the future will, in speaking of the present time, say, 'In those times they had Pavlowa.'"

She recognized talent and good interpretation only in dancers she wished to have with her or who were already in her organization; otherwise she always found something to criticize, especially if they were good, but if they were mediocre she would find a quality somehow which she would say could develop.

In speaking of materials for costumes she always said that one should employ only that which would give the result one wished to obtain, which is very true. But she was very inconsistent in following this out, for if the material was of a price very high, she bought something not so costly, saying, "It is good enough for the American public," whom she did not hold so great in esteem. Many times I have seen her laughing in the wings after leaving the stage, telling us that she had seen in the audience some people chewing gum very slowly while doing an adagio and with great speed when she was executing an animated variation.

Although she owned a home in London, she planned to buy one on the Riviera in France; when she retired she would choose to live there, but she esteemed most of all the public opinion of St. Petersburg, and preferred above all other countries to dance in Germany.

A man who was always in the background was Monsieur Dandré, her personal manager. When Diaghilew presented his ballet headed by Karsavina and Nijinsky, he boosted himself; but Dandré, the originator of the Pavlowa enterprise, eliminated himself completely and made himself absorbed by Pavlowa's personality. He was a man very learned and of an excellent Russian family in spite

Pavlowa Intime

of his name of French consonants. He was a perfect gentleman and a diplomat of great spirit and fine character. Monsieur Dandré was always there in the company to guide and to keep harmony at times when so badly needed. He watched over the career of Anna Pavlowa with a knowing and far-seeing eye. He was the power behind the throne. Much of her great success in the dance, aside from her own great genius, must be attributed to him who so admirably guided her.

I take pleasure in rendering these lines of tribute to Monsieur Dandré, who did personally for Pavlowa what Diaghilew did for the Russian ballet in general.

Cecchetti

As CLUSTINE had been the principal Ballet Master of the Imperial school of Moscow and had a pension from the government, occupying himself later with a place analogous to the Opera of Paris, Cecchetti likewise was of the Imperial school of St. Petersburg and Diaghilew had engaged him to be with him.

Pavlowa, quitting Diaghilew and forming her own troupe, took with her the best male dancers she could entice from Diaghilew, such as Mordkin, Novikoff, Zaylich and Kobeleff. She took also Cecchetti, the ballet master, with her.

Cecchetti was of Italian origin and was the possessor of all the old traditions. He was truly extraordinary, for in spite of his great age he could execute and demonstrate the most difficult steps. Only *he* refused to advance with the times and was obstinate in holding to the manners of the old routine.

At our commencement in London when I had hurt my foot he had been most kind, but later his regard for me seemed to change. My tendency to love the modern and art more advanced did not accord with his old conceptions and the success that I obtained with the dances which Clustine had taught me still further aroused his antagonism. The interest that Monsieur Zaylich showed in my dances did not please him either, and his *protegée* pupil who accompanied him, a young French girl, was another cause of his dislike—we, both speaking French, often talked together and he resented our friendliness.

CECCHETTI

It was curious, but to him even Pavlowa was not a good dancer. I recall that one time after a rehearsal of "*Giselle*" where Pavlowa had marvelously interpreted a mad scene Cecchetti criticized her work, saying, "She really looks like a lunatic. Oh, you should have seen—," (I forget the name, unknown to me, which he cited) "*that really* was a dancer." This reflection displeased me, coming from him, for she truly portrayed the character. What he said was unkind and unjust but unintentionally a compliment. I do not know whom the other dancer was but, knowing his conventional taste, am certain that she could not have been superior to Pavlowa. Furthermore, it was discourteous for him to so express himself, being in her employ.

He also criticized Nijinsky a great deal, saying that his arrangement of "*L'Apres Midi d'un Faune*" was absurd. I had seen Nijinsky myself in this interpretation and I certainly failed to agree with this criticism of Cecchetti's. I did not agree with the conception of the costume by Bakst which he wore because to me it represented more a centaur than a faun; it looked to me more like a horse with the Polka Dot than a furry faun. The stains of purple make-up gave to me the effect of a skin disease which one can see reproduced on the wax doll of the musée at the fair of Neuilly. The costumes of the women were a true find of Bakst; the first time that such Grecian conception was portrayed on the stage. The choreography of Nijinsky was excellent; very artistic in his conception of stiff archaic. Of course the faun obviously had obscene suggestive gestures, but no more than you can find in the old French "*Can-Can.*" If Nijinsky was hissed for his faun it was principally because of the last posture, restrained though it was; this last posture could suggest nothing to the innocent and could teach nothing new to those already initiated into the mysteries of love.

Paris was shocked by the *Faun* as was the preceding generation shocked by "*Carmen,*" the history of the "*fille publique*" and of a soldier-deserter. It was not the music or the beauty of the spectacle which was criticized, but a vague of pruderie that arose and caused much talk.

Diaghilew, as a true *Barnum,* at the first performance of the Faun, regardless of the hisses, immediately repeated the ballet. It was the cause of so much noise in the hall that the dancers, not being able to hear the music, were forced to guess when to do their dances. And there was much discussion about it among people and in the press. Diaghilew, however, came to establish his *Faun,* but later made a concession to the censure for some modification. I can truly say that this performance of the faun was unlucky to the general advancement of the art of the ballet. The great curiosity aroused in the public by the faun made it an attraction that brought big receipts to the box-office. Diaghilew, taking this cue, produced different works with the aim to arouse the protestations of the public and then playing on their curiosity with the result of getting crowded houses. It was effective. But following this tactic to surprise the public came the decline of the Diaghilew organization.

Returning to Cecchetti—as professor he was excellent. Being not very well disposed toward me, he criticized me on all possible occasions. It made me work harder to obtain perfection. Pavlowa was almost always there to take her lesson and her corrections from him. It was most interesting. But if by chance she was not there Cecchetti gave all his attention to his French protegée and the lesson lacked interest for the rest of us; we had to work by ourselves.

Cecchetti was truly a type one sometimes meets in life but who seemed more a character from the works of Balzac, Flauber or Dickens. I have never met anybody who could so easily work themselves into a passion and swear in Italian and completely lose themselves apropos of nothing. One day on arriving in a small town there were no taxies at the station to meet us, so we had to take a street car. Monsieur Dandré said to me, smiling, "It is curious, the day has almost passed without Cecchetti having uttered a complaint." He had hardly finished speaking when we heard a piercing and loud protest. A woman coming through the car had stepped on Cecchetti's foot. He swore in Italian as though he were being killed. We could not restrain from bursting into laughter.

The Gavotte which Clustine had arranged proved to be such a success that it became part of all the programs. Pavlowa danced wearing sandals with high heels. Before arriving in Chicago, Pavlowa twisted her ankle; dancing on a defective board had caused the trouble, but Cecchetti ascribed it to the high heels, blaming the *Gavotte.* Cecchetti held that it was bad for her to go from the high to the heel-less ballet slipper; that it was absolutely absurd for one who was a classical dancer to execute this type of dance and strange that a master of the ballet had dreamed of creating one for a ballerina. However, he was not a bad person.

I remember that Pavlowa's anniversary occurred when we were in New Orleans. The company had planned as a whole to present her with a gift and to give her flowers individually. We all assembled in the court of the theatre and Cecchetti, in most appropriate words, presented the gifts to Pavlowa in the name of the company. This scene of the old professor so happy in doing the honors to his celebrated pupil, universally recognized as a great star, seemed to me quite touching.

The setting was more than modest, contrasting singularly with the group gathered there to felicitate a great celebrity. The walls were dirty and dilapidated; the flowers were all arranged in the center, giving the effect of a grave. I often ask myself if this scene was a manifestation of Glory.

Incidents on Tour

NOT KNOWING the English language at this time made it difficult for me to be alone. In Europe there are always interpreters in the hotels and, too, their system is different from the American. There, if one is in need of something, a ring of the bell will bring a servant. If not understood one can explain by pantomine what is wanted. In America they respond from the office by telephone; a nasal voice like Punch and Judy asks something, and for one not knowing the language it is an embarrassing situation. So I really needed someone to be with me.

Andreas Pavley had lived in London and spoke fluent English and French. He was quite young, very artistic and very cultured. We were in accord in our approval of the new movements of the dance, so we were together a great deal, later becoming true friends. He had one fault. He was excessively slow in putting his effects in order after a performance.

In Salt Lake City it was announced that we were to leave immediately after the show. Pavlowa had ordered a special train to take her coaches to an intersection and there it was to be connected up with the regular express. As I never eat before dancing, I told Pavley that I would not wait for him and would join Bergé and Mademoiselle Plaskowieczka, the premiere danseuse, to go with them to supper. I was always very exact and on time for all that had to do with my work.

We supped quickly and went on to the station, but our surpise

INCIDENTS ON TOUR

was great to find that we were not at the right one. On the bulletin at the theatre when they do not indicate a new station it means that we are to depart by the one we came by. They had not done this so we had to hurry over to the other one, only to learn that Pavlowa's train had gone. What to do! We were nonplussed. How to join the train! We could telegraph to hold it at the next station, but even that would not give us the possibility to catch it. Taxies were too slow and airplane service did not exist at that time. No train was due to connect with the express. We knew of nothing that we could do and each of us was necessary for the performance—Plaskowieczka for her dances, Bergé for the *Gavotte* and I for the *Fantasie Oriental*. What could we do? We were still nervously discussing the situation when all at once we saw Pavlowa's train returning for us. What a relief! They had noticed our absence and had come back. We jumped on the train, and happily made connection with the regular express.

Another time we were to give a matinee in Washington and that same night a performance in Baltimore. The train was delayed owing to snow and weather conditions. We arrived in Baltimore late; the audience was already seated in the theatre. The arrangement of the house being bad, the stage setting and all had to be hauled right in before them. The show was two hours late. Before the presentation, Pavlowa appeared before the curtain to explain the cause and make apologies for the delay, "a little late," she said. This "a little late" made me laugh when the performance started at the time it should have been over.

There were times when celebrities were in the hall; I recall, for example, in Los Angeles, Ruth St. Denis and Mary Pickford being there. I had never seen Ruth St. Denis dance at that time, but I had heard much talk of her. Having just finished dancing the *Oriental Ballet* I bowed to her first, in respect to her great artistic reputation. I had the pleasure later of seeing her dance and sincerely admired her genius. Surely, with Isadora Duncan, she is one of the great figures in the dance and does honor to America, her country. Loie Fuller also showed originality and personality in her dance, but to me she seemed to be less prominent than Duncan and St. Denis.

Mary Pickford wore a dress giving the impression of a "petite-fille" with white gloves accentuating her heavy wrists. She had a mass of blonde curls like a Louis XIV wig, looking like a doll of papier maché. I was astonished on seeing her that she could be the ideal of the American public. She recalled to me an image d'Epinal.

Novikoff and Pavlowa had an argument which brought about his refusal to dance at the evening's performance. As Pavley had auditioned in London in a bacchanale arranged to the music of Glazounow, Pavlowa, who used this same music for her dance, chose him to perform with her. He danced marvelously; it was an enormous success and they were encored repeatedly. The next day peace was made so she performed again with Novikoff, because he was the regular partner in that dance.

A curious incident took place in St Louis. I believe the manager who had charge of Pavlowa was having some legal difficulties; I forget just what the trouble was, but through some error they put the blame on Pavlowa and seized the scenery and the costumes. She was not to blame but was put in an embarrassing position as she was booked for a show in the next town the following day. Happily, all her properties had not been seized, as part had been sent in advance to the next town, which allowed her giving the two ballets as it was the custom to give on each program. But, as to the divertissements, that was another story. Pavlowa had no doubles for them. A great many changes had to be made in the numbers, making use of some rarely used in the possession of Pavlowa.

As we were short of divertissements, Zaylich asked me to dance my Persian dance with the Clustine arrangement as a number on the program. I could not dance the Zaylich arrangement as they had been giving the ballet *Oriental Fantasy* and these two dances had to be different. I had also to wear a different costume; luckily I had one of my own. The music cut, not being the same, the general effect would not look similar. Unfortunately, after deciding all this, Maestro Stier, the conductor, announced that he had not Clustine's arrangement and that it was impossible to rearrange the music I used, that being used for the dance in accord with the arrangement of Zaylich's. What to do? There was no time for rehearsing. Everything had to be done on the moment. So I danced my *Persian dance,* the steps Clustine had taught me in the parts where the music corresponded to his arrangement choreographic; the other parts I had to improvise, being careful not to use any of the steps Zaylich had originated for his arrangement in the Oriental Fantasy.

In spite of the fact that my dance was very well received, I came from the stage covered with perspiration, not caused by fatigue but from the nervous strain I had been under, not knowing from moment to moment what I would have to do.

The following day we received our scenery and our costumes and I was happy not to be put to that test again.

The Stolen Part

"Pour un ane enleve deux laronts se bataient."
(For a stolen donkey two thieves have a fight)

THIS IS the beginning of a fable of La Fontaine, who explains in his verses where a third thief appears and appropriates the donkey during the argument.

The following incident recalls this situation to me:

For a certain spectacle given with an opera, Pavlowa had presented the *Dance of the Hours* from *La Gioconda*. She appeared as the personification of the "Night" in a black robe covered with stars. The part was very difficult and fatiguing, so after doing it once she decided to give it to some one else to do. As it was a classic dance, by right it should have been given to Mademoiselle Plaskowieczka, premiere classic dancer. But Mademoiselle Gachewska, premiere character dancer, was very friendly with Monsieur Zaylich, who arranged the ballet, and she wanted the part. This was an embarrassing position and he would not decide in favor of either of them.

To dance on toes for men is very rare, and it appears that it is the first time in the annals of the dance that one used bare feet for toe work as I do. Zaylich gave this part to me, so using toe slippers in this dance it became very easy play for me, giving the effect of floating in space. My costume was of course entirely different from the one Pavlowa used. I had black wings which gave the

Serge Oukrainsky in the ballet, Oriental Fantasy.

effect of a bat. The effect produced was most dramatic and was a great success. I was content to have this number added to my repertoire, although a bit embarrassed, having taken it from the two premiere dancers. But they did not seem to hold any resentment. There was a certain rivalry between them, so this arrangement seemed to satisfy them both.

Pavlowa had expressed the desire of dancing a "pas de deux" Egyptian with me, a dance she had never danced but with Nijinsky. She had sent for special music by Arensky, but it was drawing to the end of the season and the music did not come.

Pavley, on his side, was the best in the company in the line of Grecian and plastique dancer. He had made enormous progress also in the classic under the tutelage of Cecchetti. As character dancer he had greatly surprised Markovsky, who directed him in this branch. His progress had been rapid. He had become a splendid artist.

One time, between towns, on the train Pavley showed to the fellow artists of the troupe some excellent articles from the papers that the critics had written about him in London and other parts of England. Pavlowa approached, but having thrown a glance over the writing, went on quickly vexed.

I was surprised at her lack of interest in developing the talents of the members of her own organization. She concentrated her attention only on herself. Something written at one time must have caused her to change and made her cross and peevish, because she never read the criticisms in the papers about herself.

A certain silk concern made her a present of a new chiffon, demanding in return that she give her name to this special quality She accepted and had me aid her in the arrangement of a Greek number and designing the costumes. She had chosen the *Beautiful Blue Danube* of Strauss as the music.

I gave her the idea of employing Andreas Pavley in this number, knowing that he did so well in this genre of dance. The divertissement consisted of a dozen girls and only we two men. It was a bit of compensation for Pavley, getting way from the bacchanale and giving him an opportunity to attract again the attention of the public on him.

Pavlowa was satisfied with the success of this number, but was provoked that she had to buy about as much more of the stuff as she had been presented with. She was also very disagreeable during the rehearsal of this number.

I had designed the costumes in such a fashion that four young girls carried "des peplumes" which were unrolled and wound up on them during the dance. This is not done much by male dancers (to manipulate veils) and I became entangled in handling them at rehearsals. She said, ironically, "He calls himself an artist and cannot even unroll a scarf." I have never made any pretention to justify this remark from her and surely her reprimand was unjust as this was not anything that I was supposed to know, to manipulate chiffon.

She explained one thing that was very true and of interest to a dancer: A veil must become part of yourself, having the suggestion of being an extension of your person and to hover over you.

We returned to New York and played at the Manhattan Opera House before embarking. Isadora Duncan was at the Metropolitan and I went again to see her. If she had impressed me lightly before, I found her admirable at this time. It seemed to me a pose, dancing after the tragic deaths of her first two enfants at their funeral and with all the talk that followed showed a deplorable taste. When I saw this spectacle my opinion changed entirely, and later in reading her memoire they further strengthened this opinion. She appeared a mature woman less as a dancer than as a mime and plastique. Her dance was the interpretation of a Niobe disconsolate. It would have been impossible of anyone who had not suffered a great loss to express as she did the grandeur of such sorrow. Isadora Duncan was truly sublime. The grief of this modern Niobe made Duncan shine in a glorious aurora of a martyr.

We left the United States, going on to Germany. In America

The Stolen Part

Pavlowa had shared the honors with Bergé, Novikoff and with me. I asked myself if it would be the same in Europe. Suddenly we learned that, for a reason I ignore, Pavlowa and Novikoff had renewed their quarrel and if I remember rightly he did not appear at the last farewell performance. On the boat they did not speak to one another and we learned that he had severed his connections with the company.

Our destination was Bremen, but I asked permission to leave the boat at the French port where they stopped and then later to rejoin them in Germany. I wanted to visit with my father and see again some of my friends in Paris.

Clipping of the Dresden "Zeitung," May 19, 1914.

Clipping of the Dresden "Nachrichten," May 19, 1914.

Copy of program, opening performance in Berlin, Germany.

Germany

PAVLOWA PLANNED to take about a two months vacation after her season in Germany. She planned to spend it in Russia.

As my father was so worldly, loving the great names and the celebrities, I was sure that he would be enchanted to receive Pavlowa at his chateau, so I invited her and Monsieur Dandré to be our guests. I would speak to my father of this when in Paris. They both accepted my invitation, but when I saw my father he said it would be impossible.

There had been great trouble in Russia the last time that he had been there. While resting with some friends on the terrace of the chateau they had been fired upon. There was a spirit of revolution in the villages so, he did not even stay on his own estate but went to the nearest town and, having arranged his affairs, he returned to Odessa where he stayed in a hotel.

He much regretted all this, for he would have loved to have entertained here for them. I regretted too, for a sojourn of a month or two at our home would have given me the opportunity to exchange ideas on subjects and choreographies with Pavlowa.

I had spoken to her of the ballet "*La Peri*" by Ducas, which I thought would be most adaptable to her. It needed but two personages. It would give her the opportunity of doing a very beautiful modern work and the success would be shared with only one other as was done in her "pas de deux". This ballet was also done in the

Germany

genre that I loved and we could have worked it out together in our leisure time.

On tour she was always so occupied that it was impossible to find time to discuss a work of such importance. Even the *pas de deux Egyptian*, the music of which had arrived at the end of the tour, had not been rehearsed. It was always lack of time or fatigue.

As each cloud has its silver lining, I was happy that my father would not expect me now to go to the country place in Russia where the monotony of the steppes tired me profoundly.

Pavley was discouraged by the lack of attention that Pavlowa showed in his regard and disgusted at the banality of his repertoire. He had a contract with her for another year, and planned to leave when that time was up.

My time was up, and I, having gotten over the incident of the Metropolitan and being no longer a member of the organization, I had conferred with Monsieur Dandré and had renewed my contract for one more year; I had even obtained better arrangements. I was to receive a much larger salary, was to be employed exclusively for my specialties and there were some other privileges.

My father let me depart without opposition. He was sure that without a doubt we would meet in Vienna. He would pass through there on his way to Russia. Pavlowa would give her performances there after touring Germany.

I made a very short stay in Paris, going from there to join Pavlowa and Company at Bremen and where I had a great disappointment awaiting me.

Novikoff having quitted the company, Pavlowa had distributed the parts she had danced with him to other members of the company. The ballet of *The Magic Flute* and one of Weber's she had given to Bergé. The Bacchanale she gave to Pavley. Two other ballets and some divertissements to Kobeleff, and to me absolutely nothing.

The ballets which Bergé had received did not interest me much. I would have been pained to have received them. The bacchanale given to Pavley was only his due as he had distinguished himself before in its execution. One of the ballets and the divertissements that went to Kobeleff affected me no more than those given to Bergé. There was only one of those given to him that caused me great regret not to have received. It was *Les Preludes*.

In contrast to the usual repertoire, artistically mediocre of Pavlowa, this was a very interesting ballet. The music of Listz carrying this beautiful symphonic poem on which Michel Fokine had adapted a choreographic very modern, which he had adapted to my "genre." It was an alliage of ballet technique with postures *Heleniques and Boticelliques*. The costumes and decorations also in this style, but of a modern taste, were designed by the genial artist, Boris Anisfeld. Of all the Russian artists equalling and rivaling Bakst, Boris Anisfeld surely was at the head.

Bakst, being fortunate in the great publicity that he had received, was very popular. He had also in his favor a brilliance of coloring and a barbarism of conception *rafinée*. But Anisfeld had a technique of coloring also personal and brilliant. The one played on contrasts, the other on harmony. With Anisfeld the lines were less bizarre but more gracious. The ferocity of the others seemed to be replaced by love. In spite of this contrariness one would say that they were of the same school with the difference of their respective personalities.

The ballet *Les Preludes* was not a great success for the reason that it was too advanced for the epoch and to the public that Pavlowa had the habit of attracting. This ballet had even been booed at St. Petersburg where the taste of the public was very demoded and they only appreciated the virtuosity of the dance from the acrobatic viewpoint. It was the epoch before Diaghilew, but now ballets were showing a new form of conception.

In London, before a more educated and advanced audience, this ballet had been well received, but Pavlowa did not love it because she was not the sole attraction in the scene as she was in the old ballet of the genre of the Italian school. She was the principal figure, and could distinguish herself, as she had more to do than

GERMANY

the other participants. But according to her, she was too much a part of the picture.

It was the interpretation of a symphonic poem admirably reproduced as of a beautiful animated mural decoration. There was not the variation for the leading ballerina to hold herself on her toes as a puppet on a music box or a monkey dressed on a Hurdy Gurdy. As in the composition of a beautiful fresco the members of the ballet were admirably grouped and were not in set lines, immobile, when the premiere danseuse did her pirouetting. I was hurt that they had not given me this ballet; not because of any success I expected from it but for the personal satisfaction of interpreting a real work of art, a thing rare on the programs of Pavlowa.

An unexpected compensation came—something I was far from expecting. If I had success in America I cannot compare it to this that I won in Germany. The *Fantasy Oriental* which I danced with the arrangement of Zaylich's obtained the same success that I had received at the Metropolitan with the arrangement of Clustine's. I cannot imagine what would have happened had I danced his arrangement. However, it was of short duration. One could not be allowed to completely take all the honors from the ballet so it was arranged to change the program in a way that would be to my disadvantage.

It could not be a question of changing my dance again, having done it that way during all the American tour. Consequently, this is the change that they made: my dance was placed almost at the commencement of the *Oriental Ballet*. This ballet had always been done in the second scene, as it was very gorgeous, and this being the best place on the program, but now it was put in the first scene. My dance being at the commencement instead of toward the middle of the program in which it always attracted so much attention cut my success three-fourths. With this arrangement I finished almost at the beginning of the spectacle. The late comers did not see me dance at all, those coming in a little late distracting the attention

GERMANY

of those already in their seats. So by the end of the program my performance was but a dim memory.

I regretted that I had renewed my contract for another year.

I consoled myself by the thought that the year following Pavley and I would both be free and we could then give the beautiful works and carry out our dream of creating new and personal dances.

To add to my discontent, Monsieur Dandré announced that he had sent for the dancer T of the Imperial Theatre of Moscow to come and dance the greater part of the repertoire as Pavlowa's partner. Constantin Kobeleff was of the Imperial Theatre also, but he was too small in figure to be her partner. Pavley, Bergé and I had filled the role perfectly; no one seemed to remark about the absence of Novikoff. However, we evidently did not satisfy Monsieur Dandré, because we were not of the Imperial Theatre. Pavley was Dutch and Bergé, French.

I had the same technique as the dancers of the Imperial Theatre as I had received all my training under Clustine, but I was not a graduate of the school. However, I had the advantage over them, having had my choreographic education scrutinized "a la Loupe" by Clustine and my taste developed by a superior education and by my long sojourn in Paris. I wondered what this new dancer would be like and what effect his coming would have upon us.

Sketch by Malvina Hoffman of Serge Oukrainsky in the Boccherini Minuete, Pas de deux with Pavlowa.

Contentment

EVEN THOUGH my dance in the Oriental ballet had been again sacrificed I had, happily, some numbers in the divertissements where I could show what I could do. One number, *The Serpent and the Bird,* was again for me a delightful surprise. It had been well received in America, but in Germany it was sensational! After giving this dance in Dresden, the hall shook with the applause. I quote some of the articles in the papers in reference to the performance. The *Neueste Nachrichten* wrote, "The young Oukrainsky, who gave an interpretation of a serpent, is not only on a par with the great and celebrated Nijinsky by his individual and forceful pantomime, but he is a rival of Pavlowa herself in a fashion astonishing in the technique of his dance—for example in the virtuosity in his toe." It was signed August Puringer. The other principal newspaper of Dresden had an article signed R. S., and ran thus: "A particular note has been touched by Oukrainsky in his representation of a serpent charming a bird. It evoked an echo of the demoniac magic and of the mystic beauty of Nijinsky witchcraft, but Oukrainsky has the advantage of the graceful expressiveness of his youthful and more beautiful and harmonious body." These criticisms made history for me. Dresden was recognized as the most artistic and the most discriminating city in Germany and to have such eulogies written of me there filled me with great joys, especially as it had been an honest criticism. I having never met them personally.

I had attained my aim—to be compared to Nijinsky and by

CONTENTMENT

the most serious and competent of critics. In America I had never received such praise but they, not yet having seen Nijinsky, could not have made a comparison. All my hard work now seemed to me to be recompensed. I had had good articles, but never such as these. I was truly happy then. I was very young, not unpersonable, and with the prospect of having some day a very large fortune. Playing with great success in my first engagement and compared to Nijinsky, who was recognized as the greatest dancer in the world, I forgot all the hardships that I had gone through and had no doubt that this would last, not realizing how short it was to be, that soon the entire world would turn into chaotic barbarism, flinging civilization back a few centuries.

The Dancer T

THE DANCER T arrived from Moscow. He was a very amiable man and proved from a start a most agreeable comrade, but unfortunately he was of a certain age and had a surplus of embonpoint. He was a perfect technician and Pavlowa took from members of the company the parts she had given them and gave to T the place as successor to Novikoff.

I had thought that perhaps Pavlowa, not giving me other parts in the repertoire, would have had me fill this place to avoid the inconvenience of taking them back.

The result of confiding the greatest part of the repertoire to the dancer from the Imperial Theatre was disastrous. Although a most excellent dancer, he was ridiculous in the romantic roles of the ballet. Only his technique and the presence of Pavlowa with him saved him from being booed.

The *Bacchanale,* always encored in America with Novikoff and repeatedly encored with Pavley in Germany, now provoked but a laugh from the audience. Without doubt Pavlowa, due to contract or scruples, did not take this part from him but had to withdraw the number from the program. After his solo performance coming from the scene he received not the least applause and Monsieur Dandré, arriving just then, asked who the dancer was. They responded that it was T and he appeared surprised and very annoyed. It was truly lamentable to see the great success of the spectacle thus demolished—it had been making strides before the advent of this first dancer from the Imperial School.

Pavlowa, however, had great need of a dependable partner, for in her dances she abandoned herself completely, risking each instant disaster, a chance of being crippled for life unless her partner was there to do his part at the right moment.

Pavlowa, in her dances, showed an audacity and a boldness that I have rarely seen equalled. One time en scene it seemed to me that an accident could not help but happen—her abandonment was absolutely complete. So it was necessary in this type of dance to have a partner absolutely sure of himself and one of great experience. T sufficed these and in the ballets where he did not represent a prince charming he was acceptable. His position, though, was lamentable. He had come directly from Moscow, where the taste of the public was less developed and where he was a favorite.

In our days the American cinema have habituated people everywhere to have the performer look the part portrayed, but at this time, and above all in Russia, the public had little discrimination and a Violette in *Traviata* could weight two hundred pounds if she had a beautiful voice, as it would also allow a good dancer have the appearance of a distended "baudruche" if he correctly executed a variation.

We had such a pity for T, realizing his discomfiture, for he was not pretentious. He knew his work thoroughly and should have been put in charge of the ballet but never appear as a dancer.

Happily for him, we left Germany to continue our tour in Austria-Hungary. There the public seemed more in his favor and he was not so disappointed.

We visited Bucharest, Budapest, Prague, Vienna and other cities. I was less a favorite in these countries. They were more old-fashioned, being interested only in Pavlowa; nobody else mattered.

I did not conserve the good remembrance of those times, for I had some personal disappointments. These had nothing to do with my profession, but were enough to turn my thoughts from the dance.

The Dancer T of the Imperial Theatre

The only interest that I had was to visit the art galleries and the museums.

My father was in Vienna on his way to Russia when we played there. He came to see our spectacle. I was very much amused when presenting him to Monsieur Stier, Pavlowa's musical director. "I am very happy to make your acquaintance, Monsieur Oukrainsky," Maestro Stier said. I corrected him, telling him that that was only my professional name and that it was the first time my father had had it applied to him. We all laughed heartily at this incident.

One evening I expected to meet my father on coming out of the theatre. He was to take the express that night for Russia but, fearing to miss the train, did not wait for me. We were thus parted, never imagining that it would be more than a dozen years before we would see one another again. Such is life.

During our tour one of the men of the ballet fell ill and could not appear in one of the spectacles. If I retrace this event it is to render homage to Cecchetti and to show how devoted he was to his art. They had just given a ballet with horrible music. It was the ballet of Paquita. Maestro Stier had in vain implored Pavlowa not to give it. In this ballet there was a figure to dance where everybody was occupied and the presence of the ill dancer was indispensable for the formation of the figures. Cecchetti alone was free, so without hesitating an instant the great master took the place of the lowliest in the ensemble and so saved the play. It showed how much he reverenced his art. Cecchetti received a fine offer from Diaghilew to return to him and Pavlowa was disconsolate at the loss. There was a rivalry between the two organizations for his services. In talking to Pavlowa, I gave her a hint to approach Clustine and see if she could engage him for her next tour.

The position that Clustine had at the Opera of Paris was good, but the remuneration was not a great deal. She could make him an offer more advantageous. She had before her eyes in Bergé and in me examples of his instruction. He had, before our engagement in London, arranged a suite of dances for her entitled *Chopiniana*. They were well received.

Pavlowa said that she had thought of making him an offer, and would be pleased if he would accept. As the athletes, she desired to always have a trainer. No matter how perfect her dancing was, she saw always the possibility of doing better.

Quitting Austria-Hungary, to my great delight, we returned to Germany and terminated our tour in Berlin. From there we dispersed for about two months to meet again in London to begin a new tour.

Presentiments and Omens

As I HAVE a bad memory for names and as I have not kept notes, I just write these things as I remember them.

In a certain German city there was to be celebrated a great national fête. The emperor Wilhelm II, himself, was to be there. The baptism of a nephew or a grandson was to take place.

For this occasion Pavlowa had been engaged to give a great command performance for the Emperor and his court. The hotels in that town were filled to their utmost capacity. There was not room for another soul.

I thought that things had been very badly arranged, for expecting a big company they should have made arrangements for housing them, but nothing had been done, consequently the artsits had to seek for themselves and found places almost unimaginable.

As to myself, I, after seeking all day, found a chamber over a coach house or stable. It had been put up for rent for this occasion at a high rental. Where the stableman, these being his quarters, found a place to sleep only God knows. I did not want to run the risk of sleeping under the "beautiful stars," so was glad to have found this place.

I was very fatigued, so was happy to go to bed. I was almost asleep when a great number of soldiers passed under my window. They were, without doubt, returning from parading and maneuvering and they marched with a heavy and regular tread.

By a curious twist of mind I recalled my sojourn at the Lycée, where the professor in history periodically told the pupils of the

Presentiments and Omens

bad treatment accorded the French in Alsace Lorraine. This was periodically the culture of hate infused in young minds, this lesson was not purely educational. Although adoring Paris and France, Germany pleased me also. Being Russian, I had nothing to do with the controversy. I recalled, also, the obvious bad taste of the unforgiveness demonstrated by putting mortuary crowns on the statue of Stratsburg on the Place de la Concord. The name alone of that place should have prohibited such a demonstration and somebody with artistic inclination for the architectural beauty of this place should resent to see it transformed into a graveyard, similar to the Père Lachaise.

I remember also this propoganda of hate bearing fruit in the hisses and boos which greeted the picture of the Kaiser Wilhelm II when shown in the cinema houses in the news reels.

Here, the culture must have been the reverse. The heavy rhythm of steps which had been reaching my ears gave me the impression to crush young Frenchmen and to go straight to their mutual downfall.

Here in this stable the hate between the two nations filled my mind. So different from the philosophy taught by Him who was born in a stable. This was the prelude to the slaughter of the innocents.

The next evening our spectacle took place. We were all ready in advance, for we must commence as soon as Wilhelm II took his place in his special loge.

The theatre was magnificent. All the women in evening attire, covered with jewels, the men in different uniforms and some of these most brilliant.

The first ballet was the *Magic Flute*. Towards the middle of this number Pavlowa had a variation which she finished by standing on her toes, after which she had always a great and just ovation. She did not descend from her toes but to salute graciously the public, she held her poise awaiting the usual response. A silence as of death reigned; not a sound in the hall.

The etiquette of the occasion permitted no one to applaud before the Emperor had set the example, but he held himself immobile.

Presentiments and Omens

Pavlowa on her toes always kept a perfect equilibrium and had the air as of awaiting his approval. It seemed to be a question then of who would cede first, the great artist or the great power.

Even had she danced the variation badly, she would have drawn forth a thunder of applause from connoisseurs by the "tour de force" which she exerted in holding this poise without a tremor.

Leaning lightly forward, her short tarlatane aspread, from the back the effect was as of a hen with feathers irritated facing the sombre silhouette of the Emperor in the obscurity of the hall. She would force him to applaud.

The situation became embarrassing. Pavlowa ceded at last but not without showing a slight irritation to a close observer.

She had rested on her toes, without exaggeration, somewhere around thirty seconds and in the profound silence it had given the idea of an incalculable period of time. The orchestra took up its strain as soon as she had descended from her toes and the curtain went down at the end of the ballet in the same silence.

We hurried to prepare for the second scene, for the curtain had to be raised as soon as the Emperor took his seat. The entre-acte was interminable. He, without doubt, for politeness wished to give us plenty of time to rest and dress for the act.

The second ballet had the same reception as the first and passed in the same manner except for the "variation incident". The general atmosphere was all that one can imagine as being the most disagreeable. Everyone seemed enervated and ill at ease, an atmosphere as of before a storm, a glacial coldness in the silence.

I cannot say what impression I made with my dance, for it was received in the same manner.

It was not until after Pavlowa had danced her *Swan* that the Emperor decided to applaud. She was the sole performer in this dance, so he had volunteered to give response to show, perhaps, that his applause was intended just for her. After him the hall followed and gave to Pavlowa the acclaim that was her due and that she had well merited. However, this applause did not alter in anything the

Presentiments and Omens

general feeling as of a sickness over all.

The last number on the program was a Russian dance. Zaylich talked to me in advance and requested that I make an exception to my rule and dance this number. *The Prisiadka;* the bends in which are so bad for the knees. Pavlowa desired to finish the Spectacle dressed in a Russian costume, and have her whole company with her. So finished the program.

Pavlowa was commanded to come before the Emperor and the Empress to receive their compliments. She returned later to the wings and recounted how embarrassed she was. "Imagine," she said, "after having been presented, I kissed the hand of the Empress, who wore white gloves and have left a great red stain on them from the rouge on my lips."

When I heard these words, I do not know why, my heart beat violently. They seemed to presage something very serious. "This has the air of portending something very sinister," I said. "Pavlowa appearing in a Russian national costume and giving a Spectacle at an official German fête, the stain as of blood left on the hand of the Empress. I will not be astonished to soon hear of war between Russia and Germany." They laughed at my remark. Would that it had been only a laughing matter. I did not know that my prediction would be fulfilled so soon and that in the space of two months they would see it verified.

I was surprised to learn that after the presentation they proposed a bargain to Pavlowa. The administration ruling for the Spectacle proposed that she receive a compensation in the form of a decoration with the Imperial seal or to be paid in cash. It seemed to me that if they wished to decorate her for her art they should not expect her to buy this honor. Evidently on her side Pavlowa could afford to pay for it but Germany was rich enough to present it without cost.

As Pavlowa was more practical than vain, she chose to be paid. The future proved her wise, for a decoration from the Kaiser, some months later, had no more value than a rosette received at a cotillion. We then left for Berlin.

Berlin

As soon as I arrived in Berlin I went as usual to the theatre for the class under Cecchetti's direction. What was my surprise and to my astonishment when Pavlowa said to me, "You know that we two are to dance this evening the *Egyptian Pas De Deux*. At first I thought that she was joking, for after postponing and postponing this dance I was sure that she would not put it on her program at the great premiere in Berlin. "But I am not joking," she said, "I have meant to rehearse it with you on tour but we have never had the time. Now this dance is announced on the program for this evening, so we have to dance it."

"But, Anna Pavlowa," I said, "we have never rehearsed it together. This dance is entirely new to me. I have never executed it. It is not a solo where it would be possible for me to improvise if I should forget something; even the music I have never heard and I have not the appropriate costume to wear."

"That is nothing," she said, "make your arrangements. You know always how to design costumes superbly and to wear them marvelously. I am not worried about you; I know that you will do all right as to the dance with me. I will be there if you forget anything, so you need not be disquieted about what you have to do."

I had no choice but to accede. To appear at the Berlin premiere in a dance completely unknown to me and which Pavlowa had danced only with Nijinsky worried me to the extreme. I planned quickly the costume that I would wear and Pavley went out to purchase the things that I was in need of. Pavlowa, fortunately, had hers, so I had not to plan for her.

We left the class of Cecchetti to have a rehearsal. The music was a simple waltz by Arensky. I could not imagine music less appropriate. Nothing of the Oriental, suggestive of palm trees, pyramids, etc. A waltz that Pavlowa desired we do on our toes.

The dance in itself was very easy for her but there was nothing of the Egyptian in it but her posture of the body and the arms. It was a "pas de deux de ballet" with the arms angular as has been done now, twenty years later, by Mary Wigman under the title of "moderne dance".

This name of moderne dance had the prestige to attract ignorant disciples who have been hypnotized by the word "moderne" like larks are attracted by a shining mirror.

If, as in L' Après Midi d'un Faune of the same epoch and of similar movement, we had done it in bare feet or in sandals, it would have been more consistent, but I could not feel right to do this dance in toe slippers and to this music.

I applied myself to do my best, for I was happy to have been chosen by Pavlowa to do this dance the evening of her great premiere. The steps were not difficult, as I said before, but we had each to carry a torch in our hand. These torches had to be passed from hand to hand in the midst of Pavlowa's pirouetting back and forth, then reversing, and the great difficulty was the exchange of these torches at the right instant. It called for great precision.

The vivacity of Pavlowa, her spirit and her disdain of danger rendered it a most precarious thing, this passing of the cursed torches. They always seemed to be in the way, and furthermore, they were very heavy, being equipped with electric batteries.

One movement, miscalculated, could have been fatal to Pavlowa, doing a thing so precarious; this should have had days of rehearsal; consequently one hour's practice put me under a great tension.

In the afternoon I had to direct the making of my costume, even to cutting parts of it myself, and it was just about completed in time for me to wear en scene. It had to be basted on me in order to wear it. Pavlowa, when she saw me, said, "I was right, it is superb."

The dance, miraculously, passed off beautifully, without the least movement that would lead to a catastrophe.

In Berlin I had again the great success that I had had in Dresden. Both the public and the press were loud in my praise. I regretted, infinitely, that it was the end of the engagement.

The company dispersed to their respective homes. The little English girls returned to London; the Polish dancers to Poland; Cecchetti and his protegee were to join Diaghilew; Pavley left to visit his mother in Holland. I invited him to be my guest in Paris so that we could work together under Clustine during the vacation.

Monsieur Dandré asked if I would go to St. Petersburg and Moscow, that Pavlowa planned giving some extra recitals in Russia and would take with her just a few of us; the two premiere danseuses, Zaylich, Bergé, Kobeleff and myself. We all accepted.

Facsimile of a page from the Imperial passport of Serge Oukrainsky showing the family name.

St. Petersburg

I KNEW Russia of the south very well but I had never been to St. Petersburg or Moscow. Some of my oldest friends, friends since infancy the Konivalskys knowing of my coming to St. Petersburg invited me to stay with them. The Konivalsky brothers were officers and their sister had married the Count de Leontieff and lived very much in the social world in Paris, where I saw her very often. She was like a sister to me.

She was, at this time, in St. Petersburg. I was delighted to see her and also to see many other of the family friends. Many of them passed the winters in St. Petersburg, returning to their southern properties in the summer.

Among others was Madame Fon Deen. She was also a neighbor from the country and had married an officer of the Baltic provinces occupying a high post in St. Petersburg. She was an intimate friend of the Empress, who had stood as Godmother to her children. She knew the elite of St. Petersburg well.

My friends welcomed me with open arms and feted me in this, my first visit to their city. They complimented me on my success, my precocious success in my career.

We did not appear at the Marinsky Theatre, for none appeared there but those artists regularly engaged by the Imperial Theatre. Pavlowa belonged to them. Having only part of her organization with her at this time it was more like a private enterprise. She made arrangements for the showing at the theatre called Narodny Dom.

St. Petersburg

Although Isadora Duncan had danced with bare feet in St. Petersburg, Monsieur Dandré felt that it might be possible that the Emperor would come to see the Spectacle and that it would not be in good taste to dance so before him. I could not see how dancing in bare feet would shock anybody—the greater part of the peasants walked around so all summer and no one remarked about it.

Putting on toe shoes hid the exceptional faculty which I had of standing on the toe (points) without the least support. For the Oriental dance also it seemed to me to be demoded to wear the chaussons.

In this Spectacle we did not give a ballet. It was made up of the numerous divertissements.

I was not aware whether it was a matter of claque or not, but I found that the applause for all the numbers was equal. Each, without exception, were received in the same manner and this displeased me greatly as not presenting the real reaction of the public.

At the end of the Spectacle, Pavlowa received an enormous laurel wreath (crown) covered with little American flags, sent, they said, by the American consul. She received, also, a superb basket of dark red roses and another bouquet.

I returned after the Spectacle to the house of my friends where I found the Countess de Leontieff in a great rage. I could not imagine what had happened to put her into such a state. This is what I learned—I have never spoken of it until now, as it is of no more consequence.

In certain countries it is not the custom to present flowers to the male artists; in others, as in Russia, the custom is to send to the feminine artists all kinds of flowers and to the men they send only red roses, the palms and crowns.

The Countess de Léontieff and Madame Fon Deen had each sent me a tribute—one had sent the crown of laurel, the other the superb basket of red roses. These were the ones presented to Pavlowa when only the bouquet was meant for her.

There could have been no error as to whom they were meant

for, as the laurel wreath had a large ribbon attached to it on which my name had been imprinted in letters of gold, as is the custom on these occasions. They had detached this ribbon and planted the petite American flags, spreading the report that these had been sent by the American consul in recognition of Pavlowa's triumph in America.

The Countess de Léontieff said that the next day she and Madame Fon Deen were going to have the truth told in the St. Petersburg newspapers. I was annoyed to hear all this, but finally dissuaded her from carrying out this plan; it would only have been an embarrassment to Pavlowa and would have caused a great scandal, giving pleasure only to her envious rivals, of which she had many. In fact, I was rather happy not to have received the flowers personally. These two tributes were much too beautiful and conspicious and all out of proportion to my success. If it had been such as I had had at the Metropolitan in New York, in Berlin and Dresden, they would have been appropriate. In St. Petersburg my success was good but much less than that accorded Pavlowa, and for me to receive these immense floral offerings and Pavlowa a simple bouquet would have appeared ridiculous. However, I did not like the way the management did all this without consulting me. I would gladly have given my consent, had they asked me, and then I would, myself, have explained the situation to those who had been kind enough to send them to me.

During our tour I had often sent flowers to Pavlowa. I knew that she loved to receive flowers en scene. Often flowers presented one night were re-sent over the footlights the following night in the next city at her order.

I did not want an incident like this to spoil my career. It would have been impossible for me to have stayed on with Pavlowa if an affair like this had been published and spread by the newspapers. Pavlowa had too many envious people, and I would not have liked to have given them a chance to attribute to her such action, when the incident could have occurred without her knowledge.

St. Petersburg

My great difficulty was to appease my friends. They considered it a personal offense that their gifts had been so audaciously treated. It took me the greater part of the night to dissuade them from making trouble. I proved to them that I would be the first victim—that it would bring but sudden interruption to my career which I was then enjoying so highly. They finally consented to do nothing in the papers but would personally go to Monsieur Dandré and demand an explanation. So time was gained and Monsieur Dandré and I would have to find some way of appeasing their anger. Monsieur Dandré made excuses, saying it was perhaps the fault of the manager or the publicity man, but that it would be best to let the matter drop. To appease them, when we gave our Spectacle at Petergoff, he would see that I was presented with flowers identical to those that they had sent. I begged Monsieur to ignore the incident and not to discuss it with Pavlowa.

The next day at the station before leaving for Petergoff, taking the train, Pavlowa came to me and deplored and apologized for what had happened. I told her that it was my desire to have the whole incident ended. I was only sorry they had spoken to her about it as I would have preferred her to be kept in ignorance. I kissed her hand as a sign of amity—she kissed me also amicably on the forehead.

While I danced my dance at Petergoff, knowing that the flowers would be presented, I had the sensation that one has when contemplating a visit to a dentist. I had a fear of this comedy, but on my return I could truthfully tell my friends that the flowers had been received, and thus satisfy them. This, along with the White Night, had been getting on my nerves, spoiling my sojourn in St. Petersburg. Perhaps, in winter, when they don't see the sun, one can have an effect of sadness, but in the early summer the White Nights are unbearable. Coming from the theatre at night it was like twilight, and one would have the impression of having spent all the night without retiring and not being sleepy. It was truly a relief to me when we departed for Moscow.

Moscow

VOLTAIRE WROTE on departing from Holland, "Adieu canard, canaux, canailles, je n'ai trouve' chez vous rien qui vaille, je vous quitte sans regrets".

I found on seeing that country that Voltaire had been rather unjust in his pronouncement but had I his talent for writing I would indite something analogous to it of Moscow.

In spite of the fact that this city had been burned at the time of Napoleon, I had expected to find some vestiges of the old Byzantine churches with their magnificent bronze and marble and their precious mosaics.

Always in my mind's eye I see the minarets of St. Sophia of Constantinople and the beauty of St. Marco of Venice, which I have always so loved, but what did I find in Moscow? Church after church, but all built to gratify a gross and ignorant superstition, nothing erected to glorify a Christian faith. These were not the paintings of masters which ornamented the domes. These were nothing but daubs; and one was supposed to admire them. The houses, too, were ugly, plastered with all the colors as are the eggs for Easter.

I was welcomed there by many old friends and I had much to do to disguise my disappointment from them, finding their city a veritable horror.

Pavlowa danced in a theatre which was situated in a public garden, a place where music hall concerts were usually given. As we appeared surprised that she would choose such a theatre she explained that, having traveled much she considered that she could give her dance concerts any place and under any conditions, that she was noted for her spectacular representations and what they, the owners, had the habit of giving there ordinarily did not concern her in the least.

We presented the same program of divertissements that we had given in St. Petersburg. The press of that city had been good to me, but Moscow was less so, reproaching my "suppleness," holding it a fault, as not conforming to their old tradition, saying that Pavlowa had with her a dancer made of India rubber. This comparison displeased me, but I consoled myself quickly by recalling that the dancer T was their idol which gave me the impression of their taste and of their judgment.

One of my friends invited me, also Pavlowa and Monsieur Dandré, to a tea in a restaurant outside of the city, and from there we could get a panorama of Moscow. This hill was called "Mountain of the Sparrow" *(Vorobienie Gori)*. The view of Moscow was amusing. I say amusing rather than beautiful, for it was like a great mushroom nursery, like a model made in huge size, as for a plaything for a child. From far off, as in a movie set, one could accept the old frescoed plaster as a substitution for the lapis lazuli, the antique green and the porphyry. It really had no more value than pasteboard and was almost as ugly as Kieff, where the river overflowing its banks leaves, in places, little islets of dried mud, giving to the country the effect of having a scaled head.

We were on the terrace of the café; the orchestra played some Gypsy Airs, and then suddenly, in honor of Pavlowa, began the aria of *The Swan*. This caused the calling of the maitre d'hotel and a demand that he stop the playing. The director of the orchestra, very astonished and very much humiliated, said that he played it to do honor to Pavlowa. He came to the table to explain. Pavlowa told him that she preferred that he would not play this air because it brought back to her too many memories. I knew Pavlowa not to be

Moscow

a sentimentalist. I could never satisfy myself as to the cause of this. Could she really have been sincere? Or was this a pose?

After Moscow, we returned to St. Petersburg, where we would stay about ten days to give another performance. There I visited the Musé de l'Hermitage and was filled with admiration for such that I found there. But I had had enough of Russia—of Petergoff, which is the diminutive of Shoenbrun, which is itself the reproduction of Versailles; of Moscow, which was mostly junk compared to Constantinople and Venice; of St. Petersburg with its white nights which are so sad, the color a dirty grey, giving to all the aspect of a cheap panorama badly painted. My taste is spoiled for all else by the golden sun of Titian. I was in haste to return to true civilization —to return quickly to Berlin, Paris and London.

I asked Monsieur Dandré if he would release me from performing in the last Spectacle, in order that I might not have to wait ten days longer. I had an incomprehensible desire to leave. Happily he did not oppose my going.

I went to Colonel Litvinoff, who had known me since my infancy, and he went with me to the prefecture where I obtained, immediately, a new passport with my visa. I took a ticket direct for Paris and telegraphed to my father of my leaving, telling him that, having returned to St. Petersburg, it would be too much of a detour for me to go to Odessa to see him. So I quitted Russia vitally, happy to be on the train and on my way to Paris.

Little did I think, however, that I would never again return to Russia.

Anna Pavlowa, Alexander Volinine, Serge Oukrainsky in a Grecian Pas de Trois, arranged by Ivan Clustine. Photograph taken at Ivy House, London, England, from the New York Tribune, Sunday, January 24, 1915.

Vacations

I CHANGED trains at Berlin and rested there some hours. I was happy to see this city again where I had had such great success. I revisited the familiar places which I had frequented on the Friederichstrasse and then took the train for Paris.

On returning to my quarters it seemed as if awakening from a dream, all this that had occurred being so different from my accustomed life, and now that I had returned everything that I found at home seemed far away from me. I had occasions to see again the ballets of Diaghilew at the Theatre des Champs Elysée. The great epoch of the Russian ballet had passed its novelty, was wearing off. Diaghilew threw himself into this second new period, neglecting the art, seeking only sensationalism for commercial profit.

Up to now, the ballet under the direction of Michel Fokine had, in its beauty and in its novelty, kept to the classic; now, under the leadership of Nijinsky, it had broken away from that standard and took the direction to the extreme.

The first ballet of this type was *Le Sacre du Printemps,* by Stravinsky. *L'Apres Midi d'un Faune* is as a trait of union between these two periods. *The Faun* is very beautiful choreographically. It has called forth protestations only from a moral viewpoint.

After the premiere of *Le Sacre du Printemps* the press of Paris gave it the appellation of *Le Masacre du Printemps.* The music is very dissonant, very modern in conception, one very powerful, and it was truly the only thing interesting in the ballet. It portrayed the myths of prehistoric Russia. As a symphonic work it is possible to conceive its being done effectively but to see it produced before the eyes made one regret that they had good eyesight. It was truly too bad to submit such good dancers as Diaghilew then had to such a test. One could have employed for this work anyone. The decorations were ugly, the costumes more archaelogic than artistic. Karsavina had the luck to avoid the interpretation of the *Sacrificed Virgin*. This part was confined to Mademoiselle Piltz, a very good dancer, who executed exceptionally well this thankless role. The choreography of Nijinsky compelled Mademoiselle Piltz to rest an interminable time immobile in a grotesque pose (holding her cheek in her hand). The audience laughed and someone cried, "Bring on a dentist," and during all the ballet such calls came from the hall as, "Savages, go back home." Although the audience was very sophisticated, the tumult in the hall was almost as loud as the music of the orchestra.

As I have already said, the arts are all alike—and have everything in common. Take, for example, painting. We have seen the frescoes, stiltified, of Egypt. Then come the contours sensually harmonious of those of Pompeii. The primitive Italians started the trend towards new lines, gracious as of Botticelli, more stiff as Carpatchio and Bellini. Then came the sumptuous Renaissance with its Titian Michel Angelo, the superhuman execution and ironique philosophy of Léonardo de Vinci and the boring perfection of Raphaël. Commencing to descend from the summit, we come to the elegance of Watteau, the libertinage of Bouché, the naturalism of Chardin. Abandoning the artists of the XVIII cycle, we come to the cold academic school of Ingre and of David, who do not glorify the Empire Period. Gustave Doré and Gustave Moreau seem to come too late to belong to the Victorian era where we arrive at the ugly naturalism of Degat and Manet, followed by the snobbism of Picasso, arriving at the picture drawn by a donkey.

This created a famous scandal in Paris when a group of artists (indignant of ultra modern work), tied a brush to a donkey's tail

VACATIONS

dipped in different colored pots of paint, which they let him swish against a canvas. This took place before a Notary Public as witness. Then under an assumed name they sent the donkey's masterpiece to the Salon "Des Independents" under the title "Sunset on the Adriatic". After this painting had obtained notable praise of some art critics on this new-born genius, the artists made known the facts to the Paris newspapers, publishing the fact which created a commotion in the art world.

"Le Sacre du Printemps" (exception made to the music) was the commencement to the end of Diaghilew. There he began to be compelled, regardless of the production, to make novelties using much ballyhoo with the aim of attracting the populace if not the admirers, at least the curious who would pay the same price for their seats. The result of these tactics is the ballet *Parade*.

It seemed too bad to me that Diaghilew adopted this line, and that Pavlowa, too, a dancer of such great merit, should retrograde to anything banal, just in the reverse direction.

In my studio I continued my training and Clustine again came to direct his classes. Bergé was there each morning to work assiduously, and Pavley also, who was a guest in my home. We three continued our work under the supervision of Clustine.

Our lessons finished, I, acting as Mentor, showed Pavley Paris, doing the honors as best I could.

Since Pavley was Dutch, I asked Clustine, using that pretext, to design a choreography of a dance of that country for him in order to have something personal in Pavlowa's repertoire, so they worked out together such a divertissement.

We worked also on a Bacchanale to be danced with Pavlowa.

Clustine would arrange for me, too, a dance to be done with her of the XVIII century style, employing the roguish music of the celebrated minuet of Boccherini.

All went along very peaceably and we enjoyed our vacation while making our preparations for the following season's tour.

Vacations

I was becoming a little short of money. I had received nothing from my father for a year, depending solely on my earnings from the dance. I wrote him that I would very much appreciate it if he would send me some money very soon, as our season would not open for some time to come.

So it was in this condition that suddenly "all changed as a scene is shifted in a theatre".

Paris, August, 1914

I DO NOT KNOW how to undertake the task of relating this that followed. All that happened had the air of lasting an eternity, but had happened, seemingly, with the rapidity of a flash of lightning.

The events arrived pell mell, intercrossing and superimposing themselves one upon the other and then dividing into different ramifications. It seemed to me that I was entered into a new dimension in which it was impossible to conceive either the form or the immensity.

There were some rumors of war but the naiveté of my youth would not permit of my believing that such a thing was possible.

There had been in my time, I admit, some colonial wars to civilize the cannibals. I was well aware of the fact that in Russia there existed a sentiment anti-semitic, that in Turkey the Mohammedans despised the Christians; that in the United States there was the antagonism of the whites against the Negroes.

I have never been able to conceive of this spirit. I have traveled much and I have seen too many people not to know that each and all have both their good and their bad points. Being a citizen of the world and speaking the universal language of the Arts, I cannot have the prejudices of race or of religion.

"One" with a great spirit conceived the universe for all—not for just one. Then the less enlightened make a distinction of races, less intelligent came the distinction of countries, then more ignorant would make distinction of provinces, mediocre minds make even

Paris, August, 1914

distinction of towns. With the petit bourgeois it is not a question of personality but of quarters which count. A narrow-minded man discriminates even in his own family and the brute ignorant and perfect egotist tries to reduce the universe to his own proper person, believing himself to be the pivot of the world, not realizing that he is but a little atom existing not by himself alone.

I believed that the rivalry, as that of Rome and Carthage, the massacre of St. Bartholomew's Day, the hate of the Capulets and Montagues and all such things were things of the past.

I could not conceive the Emperor Francis Joseph of Austria parading in a procession of great pomp, carrying the sainted sacrament and using it to make a camouflage for a cannon.

No, I believed not in war.

Nero is considered a monster by posterity for having burned (for sanitary reasons) the pestilential quarter of Rome when he gave his own private park as a place of habitation for the refugees.

Then, what should be called the monster in this civilized age that would burn and destroy beautiful and healthful habitation and offer to Moloch a holocaust of innumerable martyrs, men, women and children, and all for commercial business reasons, for jealousy and greed.

On going to my tailor's for a fitting, this that he said disturbed me (one of his clients had sent his uniforms to be enlarged—he was an officer in reserve). "This presage is no good," said the tailor; but it was not until the next day that the great shock came.

I was tranquilly seated on the terrace of a café in the *Place Péraire,* near where I lived, partaking of an aperitif, when a mob came to read announcements on the bill-board and at the same time, a great noise of cries resounded as a band of newsboys, selling the late paper, came running and shouting, *"Mobilization Général."*

There was to be war. I now had no doubt of it. France would not give an order like this simply for a review.

At the same time the newsboys announced the invasion of Belgium by the Germans. I have had much disillusionment about

PARIS, AUGUST, 1914

men, but if they, as individuals, could break their word and forfeit their honor, I believed that a country would never do so. The fact then of the invasion of an innocent and neutral country without any declaration of war disconcerted me completely.

From then on the kaleidoscope of events succeeded one another without interruption. I did not know what to do. I grasped that it would be necessary to proceed according to all kinds of red tape, if Pavley and I, strangers, were to remain in Paris.

My passport was in order, and my father, being a property owner in the city, the thing, for me, was simple. Pavley, on the contrary, traveled as a bird of the air, without any papers of identification to prove who he was or to what country he belonged. Being of The Netherlands, speaking French well, he still had a slight accent which could be easily mistaken for German, an unfortunate situation at this time.

My being short of money and all communication with my father in Russia being completely interrupted added to the complication. The banks pronounced a moratorium, so even those who had means could not get it. All the gold was retired. One could not cash his bank notes and the market was inundated by coupons; the small money even had disappeared, postal stamps serving as exchange.

I had Pavley telegraph to his mother in Holland, requesting her to send him a copy of his birth certificate or some official paper for identification so that he could produce at the Netherlands Consulate a passport and also get a permit of sojourn. In the meantime the paper would not arrive on time for the registration by the commissaire, which must be made in the next twenty-four hours.

Happily, a friend of mine, a journalist on "The Echo of Paris," knew the commissaire of this quarter, and my papers being all right, we two vouched that we knew Pavley was Dutch and of a neutral country, and so had the right to reside in Paris. All Germans had to quit France or be sent to the concentration camp.

All individuals in time of war can easily be suspected of spying,

Paris, August, 1914

and especially such as Pavley with his German accent. I was thankful when I saw him handed his permit of sojourn.

Pavlowa sent us word that she and Monsieur Dandré had arrived in Paris. They had come on the last train to leave Germany and were going on to London.

I went to the Russian Embassy. There was an enormous crowd, all intent on doing something, like I found at the Commissioner of Police and everywhere when something had to be done compulsory and in a hurry.

Being the only son, according to the laws of Russia, I was exempt from military service but belonged to what they called the second army of reserves. To my great surprise I was compelled to be registered any way, inscribed as such in the books.

An edict was passed permitting to all Russian subjects who would be called later the choice of enlisting with the army of their own country or with that of one of the allied countries.

"Where do you desire to devote your services in case that you are called?" demanded the man in the embassy in charge of this registration.

It is curious what all can pass through the mind in such a moment of great excitement. In the space of the two seconds between his question and my response, the reasonings which I put to myself ran about like this: I reflected that in France the soldiers would be better treated than those in Russia, but that if the war was very intense the forces of Germany would surely concentrate on this side. It was probable, also, that in France they would more quickly run short of men. And then again I knew the French to be very chauvinistic and it might be possible that they would employ the stranger, so called volunteers, in the perilous positions, safeguarding their own. In Russia the soldiers would be much less well treated and the climate there is essentially severe, but they have a great reserve of men, very robust, so it might be that I would never be called. Even if they would call me, I am of a constitution rather delicate and being in my own country would run the chance of being treated with more consideration.

If I approved of war I would enroll as a volunteer, but as it is contrary to all my principles, I think it best to do all that I can to avoid it, but in an honorable way and not to be a coward.

I have never had fear of death but I dreaded physical pain and also abhorred the idea of being an invalid for the rest of my days. I would give my life with pleasure if it would save that of another, but to go and kill and be killed; to augment the number of the unfortunate in this butchery. I could not see the stupid necessity.

Then again, the war might be terminated before they would need to call me and force me to go and assassinate.

"In Russia," I answered, having in my mind more the swift vision of these reflections than their reasoning.

The man of the Embassy inscribed my response, so having fulfilled my duty, I left the Embassy.

Pavlowa gave to Pavley and to me the price of our tickets to London to join her. We could not leave with her but would rejoin her there later. Pavley had not as yet received his paper permitting him to make application for a passport. Pavlowa and Monsieur Dandré, on leaving, demanded of us that we hurry, because travel between France and England was soon apt to be a perilous and interrupted thing. It did so prove to be with the German submarines and the floating mines.

Pavlowa asked me to trace her trunk, which had not been put on the train with her. Arriving on the last train out of Germany, she thus escaped being held a prisoner, but the trunks never did arrive.

Pavley and I planned to follow as quickly as we possibly could.

I invited Pavley to be my guest during the vacation. He, too, was without money, as I was. Pavlowa had advanced money for our tickets. We could not ask her for more because she, herself, on account of the moratorium declared by the banks, had not much of which to dispose. It was but as an artiste from the Imperial Theatre

Paris, August, 1914

(with a permit of absence) that she had been able to obtain a sum for herself from the Russian Embassy.

I had in service (in my father's house) three servitors. One was the concierge—she was French, and according to the custom of Paris her remuneration consisted principally in lodgment. Her duties really consist of doing nothing except to act as *Cerberus*. But my father had ordinarily a Russian personnel for he found that they gave better service. He had taken with him to Russia the chef and the maitre d'hotel, but had left two Russian domestics in my charge and right then it was an extra responsibility.

To sell some of the furniture of the house, knowing my father as I did, I knew would be a life-long reproach from him as a crime unforgivable even though done in a time of such extreme and exceptional need. And then, again, I would have received very little for it at such a time.

The Baron Dzuilen, born a Rothchild, was an old friend of my father and of my mother, when they were in Nice, and since then it had become a custom for my father and me to dine with them, en famille, on the first of every year.

I wrote a letter to the Baroness (the baron, I heard, was absent), explaining my predicament and asking if she would not be kind enough to help me out of this temporary embarrassment. The letter received no response although it was delivered, for I had given it to one of my domestics, charging him to give it directly to her.

This rebuff turned me against addressing any other social friends of my father's. Among my own friends and comrades the greater number were not very moneyed, so Pavley and I, to economize, started in to prepare our meals ourselves. But this debut in things culinary had the result of costing more than if we went to eat at a restaurant. Happily, one of the two domestics, an excellent boy, told me that he could accept a place in the house of a Russian general who desired to have a servitor who spoke Russian. He said that he would take it upon himself to assist the other domestics until my father could get in touch with them and send for them. I thanked

Paris, August, 1914

him sincerely for thus coming to my aid, and as he was very religious, I made him a present of a superb Ikon of silver. I knew that it was a a present that would give him much pleasure. Unfortunately it did not bring luck to the poor boy. Some time later my father sent the money to him to return to Russia. He went, and as he was neither thief nor assassin, ended by being drowned by the Bolshevists.

I had, when going to the Lycée in my youth, frequented a certain restaurant and had often gone there since. I went to the proprietor of this place and asked him if he would give me credit for a certain time and also credit for Pavley, whom I presented as a cousin "de passage". I feared if I said guest he would refuse it to him.

I have not the habit of lying and have done so only on the rarest occasions, considering it a cowardice; it is only the fear to admit a personal opinion or it is to camouflage dishonest aim.

I was glad to have my two domestics off my mind and to have obtained this credit for our meals. One of my friends advanced me a small sum of money and then again another good comrade of my Lycée days. Alfred Chaskin, an American, to whom I had never dreamed of asking for a loan, proposed, himself, to come to my aid. I appreciated his great kindness, but declined his offer for I had enough to carry me through for a while.

These were the events which occurred while we were waiting for Pavley's papers to come so that we could depart (not knowing, really, whether or not we were to get them).

How great our joy when they did arrive! But how great was my stupefaction when I saw that they were in an entirely different name. Pavley belonged to a very good Dutch family and had, as I, taken a stage name.

He took his mother's maiden name, but to the commissaire he had not told this, and his permit of sojourn was in his stage name, and now came the birth certificate with his true name.

We finally came to the conclusion that it did not matter much, anyway, as we were to leave shortly. These papers would enable him to get the necessary passport which he must have to go to Eng-

Paris, August, 1914

land, so going from the consulate of Netherlands to that of Great Britain we took our two passports for the English visa.

I was in haste to leave Paris for more reasons than one. First, was the fear that transportation of passengers might be discontinued at any moment. This surely would be a final catastrophe for us, for our plan was to have another season in America.

The tour planned by Pavlowa to Germany was necessarily canceled, so she planned to give Spectacles in England, filling up that extra time before going to America.

Another reason for my desire to leave was that Paris seemed so completely changed. It seemed no more the city that I had loved, as though it had been my natal city. We could not go out without being accosted by the police officer, demanding to see our permits of sojourn. Pavley and I were both very young, so the attitude towards us was critical, as if resenting our not being at the front and as if we were undeservedly eating their bread.

However, Pavley, being of a neutral country, had no interest in this conflict, and I had registered and was in accord with the rule required by my country, an ally, and surely my father had dispensed enough money in France to warrant that I stay this short time while arranging my affairs, but I was sensitive to this antagonistic spirit.

It seemed curious, but the approach of the German troops, which were coming near, was the least of our preoccupations, although they were saying already that the city, without doubt, would have to be evacuated.

The general tension was indescribable, uplifted by an exaltation of a hysterical chauvinism.

I remember Elga P., a Dane without any personal sentiment in the conflict, upon seeing a woman conducting her husband to the station, he in uniform leaving for the front, exclaiming, all exalted: "She has a great courage," for the woman seemed insensible of the separation from her husband. I asked myself if it truly was courage. Could it be a pain so tremendous as to act as an anaesthetic on all

Paris, August, 1914

sentiment, or was she a woman seeing in the war the simplification of a divorce?

Another time, having gone to see a friend who chanced to be not at home, the concierge launched into a conversation. It was all against Germany. "Ah, if I only had hold of one," he said, "he would pass a bad quarter of an hour." I looked at him stupefied. I had not before me a civilized and debonaire Parisian but a savage of a ferocious tribe ready to martyr a prisoner from another tribe. I pictured this German that he so desired to have in his hands to torture—a big, blond German boy with eyes of blue as the *Vergess-meinicht,* not with a heart of a red-blooded murderer, but one enclosing the white flower of the Edelweiss, symbol of the German sentimentality, having left behind him a mother or a fiancée; poor sheep that a bloody Panurge could throw into his hands.

METROPOLITAN OPERA HOUSE — SEASON 1914-1915

PROGRAMME CONTINUED

Dances of Animated Dolls

DRESDEN CHINA DOLLS..........Mlle. Fredova, Saxova, Cortnova, Verina
TYROLEAN DOLL...MLLE. SVIRSKAIA
AUTOMATON LOUIS 14TH.............................M. OUKRAINSKI
CANTEEN KEEPERS.....................MLLES. BUTSOVA, GRIFOVA
JUMPING JACK..M. KOBELEFF
JUMPING JILL..MLLE. MOSKVINA
PIERROT ....MLLE. DORISOVA
SPANISH DOLL ....MLLE. KUHN
BABY DOLL ....MLLE. PLASKOVIETZKA
CHIMNEY SWEEPER ....M. PAVLEY
TIN SOLDIERS..................................MM. LOBOIKO, MARINI
FATHER KNICKERBOCKER..........MLLES. COLLINET, WORONOVA
QUAKER GIRLS.....................MLLES. CROMBOVA, LEGGIEROVA

SEVRES CHINA DOLLS:
    Mlles. Linovskaia, Schelton, Brunova, Florence
    MM. Vajinski, Zalewski, Domoslavski, Veseloff
PAS DE DEUX (Fairy Doll and Prince Charming)
    MLLE. PAVLOWA and M. VOLININE
POLKA COMIQUE..............MLLE. PLASKOVIETZKA and M. PAVLEY
MARCH AND GALLOP..Entire Company

PART II

WALPURGIS NIGHT

(Taken from the Opera "Faust")

Arranged by IVAN CLUSTINE. Music by CHARLES GOUNOD. Scenery Designed by S. SIME. Costumes Designed by L. ORLEY DE CARA. Costumes Executed by Alias, of London.

CHARACTERS

FAUST ....M. VESELOFF
MEPHISTO ....M. OUKRAINSKI
HELENA ....MLLE. PAVLOWA
CLEOPATRA ....MLLE. KUHN
FRINA ....MLLE. PLASKOVIETZKA
LAYS ....MLLE. BUTSOVA
ASPASIA ....MLLE. CROMBOVA
CLEOPATRA'S SLAVE...M. VOLININE
HELENA'S SLAVES................MLLE. SVIRSKAIA, M. PAVLEY
COURTESANS...............Mlles. Lindovskaia, Fredova, Cortnova, Saxova
NUBIANS..........Mlles. Crombova, Grifova, Leggierova, Collinet, Moskvina, Waronova, Florence
EGYPTIANS.....................Mlles. Schelton, Brunova, Dorisova, Verina
GRECIANS........................MM. Vajinski, Kobeleff, Zalewski, Loboiko
EGYPTIANS..MM. VESELOFF, MARINI

PROGRAMME CONTINUED ON PAGE 26

Page from the program of Anna Pavlowa performance at the Metropolitan Opera House in New York, showing Serge Oukrainsky as both dancer and costume designer.

Departing for London

I HAD completely given up my training during this time. The dance seemed to me to be too futile and my mind was full of other things. It astonished me to see how placidly Pavley continued with his exercises. Bergé also was calm, feeling sure of rejoining Pavlowa in England. Clustine had made arrangements with Pavlowa to take the position of Cecchetti for the next season.

Bergé was not able to go, being kept for military duty. Happily, however, he survived the war and again came to dance with her much later.

Clustine, Pavley and I concluded our arrangements for leaving. We were to take one of the last boats still running. One was not allowed to take much baggage. They allowed each passenger the minimum. Pavley and I had but two small trunks; we had our suits and a few costumes, but we were unable to send the trunks to the depot.

From the Avenue de Villier, where we lived, to the station de L'Est from which our train departed, one had to traverse all Paris. The taxies and the horses had all been requisitioned. It was a man with a wheelbarrow that we finally hired to take our baggage for us, and we had to walk with him to the railroad station.

The next day we left; we took the *Métropolitain,* having disposed of our trunks the previous day. I had never supposed that a day would come when I would be content to leave Paris, but now the crowd of people revolted me, unnerved me. I quarreled even with a

Departing for London

friend on this war question. He, anti-German and belligerent, fell into a post far from the front. I said that those responsible for war ought to be made to fight it out themselves and exterminate each other, only in this fashion could peace come to the earth.

We got on the train, after ascertaining that our trunks were there; I felt as if escaping a nightmare and hoped that all our worries were ended. But quite soon I was to experience a new anxiety.

We arrived at the pier to take our boat. The people, crowding and pushing each other, were in a state of nervousness indescribable. One cannot imagine such a scene if he has not found himself in a similar situation.

In Nice, when I was a youth, I greatly loved the gay and carefree crowds of the Carnival time, but since seeing the crowds of Paris in that time, I cannot stand them any more. Now a crowd has the effect on me as of a monster hypocrite, which seems innocent, but if demasked would appear as a reptile ready to devour implacably.

In 1870 there were murderous masses who had been shouting, "To Berlin," but it was the German troops which made their entrance into Paris. In 1914 it was the same; it was again the resurrected ghost who had been shouting, "To Berlin". The same "War Cry". The lesson had not borne fruit. Will history repeat itself?

At the gangway to the boat there was a veritable crush, a seething crowd which you could expect in time of panic. Finally, Pavley arrived in front of the officer in charge, with me just behind him. As our passports were in order, I felt there was nothing to worry about, but to my consternation I saw there a military officer having the officer verify the passports, and demand also the permits of sojourn.

Why the permits of sojourn when we were leaving? But that was what they were doing.

What to do! How to explain that the permit of sojourn and the passport, each in a different name, seemingly so incorrect were in

Departing for London

reality in order? In this time of war, with the country under martial law and Pavley with his German accent.

One who had not been placed in a like situation cannot realize the gravity of the position. With the fear of espionage it would have been possible to be shot for such a thing at a time like this. I did not believe that they would go to such an extremity but I was sure that they would keep him back—not let him go on.

Evidently, in time, with explanations and proof, it would be possible to clear the situation. But this was possibly the last boat to take passengers to England.

I could not go on without Pavley—abandon him—leave him alone in France without money and knowing almost no one. It would be necessary for me to stay also. There would be no possibility of departing for a long time and to stay in this country where they now looked upon us with reproach. What a perspective! The Germans were now already near Paris; we would be obliged, in spite of ourselves, to enroll as volunteers, or at least forced, perhaps, to join the Red Cross and act as stretcher bearers. The thought of all the abominations one would have to see would certainly drive me to suicide.

The people cried impatiently at the length of time given to the verification of these papers by the official. Pavley presented his passport to the officer; the officer inspected it and saw it was perfectly in order and then asked for his permit of sojourn.

At this moment I had an inspiration. I pushed Pavely rudely aside, making him go three or four feet from the officer, and saying something like this, "Cannot you hurry? It is all I can do to hold the crowd behind me." And saying these words, I presented my passport and my permit of sojourn at the same time, thus making the officer use both his hands.

It was true that I had kept the crowd back on the gangplank, not giving passage but to one at a time, but when suddenly I felt the way free, there was immediately a half dozen pushed forward and all trying to present their papers to the officer.

Departing for London

Pavley looked at me with astonishment. The officer said to him, "Have you your permit?" Pavley, without giving it to him, held it up, and the officer, seeing it, said, "That is all right then, go along." He never dreamed that the permit carried an entirely different name from the passport.

As both my papers were all in order, I joined Pavley, but the journey was for me one of anxiety unimaginable. The fear of German submarines did not worry me, but I kept asking myself if we would have this same ordeal to go through on landing in London.

I consoled myself by thinking that we would be on the other side anyway, and that if there was any trouble we could immediately get in touch with Pavlowa and she would come to our rescue, knowing everybody in London worthwhile.

On arriving in England there was a form to go through, but there was more order, they only demanded our passports. We quickly debarked and immediately took the train for London.

London

How HAPPY we were to find ourselves back in London. There one felt less the chaos which later enveloped the entire world. Regardless of the wartime in Europe, England seemed isolated.

Distance and time are the shock absorbers of sorrow. We stopped in another boarding house where Pavley had stayed before. Clustine was also in London, but Bergé, unfortunately, could not join us. Pavley and I continued to be without money; this was the first time in my life I had been placed in such a position and unfortunately it was not the last.

I had a very beautiful emerald which was handed down in my family. It was not more than three carats, but without any flaws and of the finest color. This stone was so perfect that the Princess Ouraussoff, the wife of the late Russian ambassador in Vienna, who was a great collector of jewels, saw me wearing it once at a dinner in her home. She began teasing me, pretending it was not real, because it was too perfect.

I gave the ring to Armand Point to have it reset, who was an artist Orphevre, and he created a design in Renaissance style, inset with a diamond ornated with green enamel. Regardless of the difficult war time, I obtained some money, pawning the jewel. Besides that, Pavlowa was making a new repertoire and after the success which the costume I had designed for her Gavotte obtained, gave me an order to make new sketches and paid me a pound for each sketch I drew for her performance of the *Walpurgis Night* of *Faust* to

London

encourage me in this new line of art. It was not much, but came very handy.

To fill up the lost time because of the cancelling of her tour in Germany, we played a few dates in Herogate and Manchester, all this put together took me out of my embarrassing position.

There were some changes in the personnel of the company. The young English girls were about the same. Mme. Plaskowieczka was also with us, but Mme. Gashewska (first character dancer) had been replaced by Mme. Kuhn. Clustine took the place of Cecchetti, Zaylich and Bergé appropriating the parts of three men. I was sorry the last two were not with us. The dancer "T" of course was not re-engaged, but Pavlowa engaged Volinine instead. Of all the classical dancers I have seen or met, including Nijinsky, Volinine is the one who possessed the best technique and who danced the most correctly. In point of view of the school of the dance, he is superior to all. The only reproach you could make was, "He is simply a dancer. He has no different style beside the classic, he does not create a character or execute a dance artistically or with individuality. He simply dances, but he does dance perfectly." He was not bad looking and he turned out to be an excellent fellow artist, without professional jealousy and ready to recognize anyone's good merit. This was a big difference from the way others have acted.

Volinine received the success he deserved and expected and he was satisfied, having no resentment if others also had success.

The attitude of Clustine displeased me greatly; he did everything in his power to train me so they could say "he had formed a dancer rivaling Nijinsky". By gratefulness I complimented him very much to Pavlowa, and Cecchetti leaving, Clustine obtained this engagement very much on my repeated praise. Now, instead of keeping himself to the position of ballet master, like his age and his figure should have advised him, or to do like Cecchetti only the roles of pantomime, Clustine wanted to be first dancer. I never could understand an artist like Pavlowa to be so lenient with him and to let him have his own way.

LONDON

Knowing that the *Gavotte* had had a tremendous success with Bergé, he obtained consent from Pavlowa to dance this number with her, which made him lose half of his success. Clustine, for the *Gavotte*, was not as impossible as the dancer "T" in Germany in the *Bacchanale*, but was far from filling all that was required. In Manchester, for example, a critic on the Manchester Guardian wrote, "In the *Gavotte Pavlowa* there was nothing immortal and forever young. It was marvelously witty, graceful, and accomplished, but, horror of horrors, middle-aged and aware of it. This was the spirit in which one of Balzac's Parisian bankers might have danced (supposing him so very fortunate with his partner), with the heights hopelessly beyond him and a full experience of 'the expense of spirit in a waste of shame' behind him. It was elegant, but somehow disconcerting." There were, in the meantime, three dancers Pavlowa could have used for the *Gavotte*. Pavley, Volinine or myself.

A Russian dancer of renown was in London at this time, Mademoiselle Tamara de Swirskaya. She had already become known in America, where she had appeared as premiere danseuse at the Metropolitan, in vaudeville and in different concert tours.

She was not a technician, but a dancer of admirable plastique line, possessing a body of marvelous contours and, more than this, was a fine musician, an excellent pianist, a graduate of a German conservatory—if I remember right, it was of Munich. She was always very smartly dressed, her clothes, which she wore most beautifully, being made by noted couturiers of Paris, where she lived between engagements.

By a curious coincidence, Pavlowa had Clustine originate a ballet along the lines of the modern ballroom dances. After the success of the Gavotte, which truly was not a gavotte of the XVIII century, but more on the genre of the dance of Irene Castle (ballroom exhibition), Clustine believed that he could create and launch these dances, that they would be adopted by the public and take the place of the fox-trot, two-step, etc.

But the result was most unhappy. The dances were not perfected

Tamara Swirskaya, formerly premier danseuse with the Metropolitan and Chicago Grand Opera Companies, at the piano.

LONDON

enough to show Pavlowa at her best and were too complicated in their arrangement, too proper to interest the present-day public as a mode of expression for themselves. There were none of the interlaced or clinch which, under the shield of hypocrisy, is so-called dance and in reality is only a flirtation accepted by our moral and which is the base of social dances. These dances neither were developed or worked out to be of great interest to the public after seeing them danced by Pavlowa on the stage. People would not give the time in the present day to study and learn to make the bows and the steps more or less complicated as they did in the XVIII century. They had neither the time or the money to pay a master for instruction in what to them was a simple pastime. Besides that, the body of the man, which comes close to the body of the woman in the waltz, now comes closer and closer, a dance which was before tolerated only in public houses, between a sailor and a fast girl, hypocritically insinuates itself in a drawing room like a low-bred person sometimes reaches high society.

I wonder if this is naivete or hypocrisy from the people, to admit in this present day that people are actually making love in public, like in times of Grecian and Roman Bacchanale, they are doing that under the banner of the dance. Poor "Terpsichore," to whom they give the position of A *Madame*. Referring to the dances of Clustine, there was nothing of this kind included and consequently could not be accepted by the public and were doomed to fail in their forgetfulness. The idea was absurd anyway, but it was the success of the Gavotte that gave birth to the thought, so the Gavotte must be held to blame.

Because of the war Pavlowa was not able to command the fashionable gowns for the ballets from the great couturiers of Paris; all work there was suddenly stopped. The dancers must be perfectly equipped—there could be no question of having costumes made in London or of buying them already made, for they must be original creations, and they could not be ordered at the costumers as they should be—special creations made by fine French dressmakers.

Pavlowa would never have dreamed of taking with her a dancer

Tamara Swirskaya wearing a gown specially designed for her by Lanvin of Paris for her concert appearances.

of repute, one having a big name like herself, as no more would Mademoiselle Tamara de Swirskaya have dreamed of accepting an engagement in a company other than her own; but under these wartime conditions things were different. Mademoiselle de Swirskaya found herself without engagements; her contracts in France and Germany where she expected to dance were automatically broken. She had a marvelous wardrobe, the latest style creations. Pavlowa, having need for just such a wardrobe for the dances in her new ballet, had Clustine, who had been instructor to them both, introduce them, resulting in the engagement of Madamoiselle Tamara Swirskaya for her specialty dance, and Pavlowa asked her the favor of ceding her wardrobe for the ballet of her modern dances.

Mademoiselle Swirskaya was truly a concert pianist, so Pavlowa introduced for her also in the ballet an interlude. It was as if in a salon one of the invited had been asked to play a piece on the piano during the reception. It was all right with Pavlowa that Swirskaya received great applause as a pianist, but had it been as a dancer it would have been an entirely different matter. So it was under these conditions and in this unexpected fashion that Mademoiselle Swirskaya signed up for her engagement with Pavlowa.

We continued our rehearsals in London and gave a few performances in other English surrounding towns before embarking for the United States. Before leaving we gave a gala performance at the Palace Theatre for the benefit of the Red Cross. The Queen was present in her box at this performance. As this was not a command affair but one given for charity, the etiquette was not the same as that given for Wilhelm II. The presence of the Queen gave more brilliance to the event with a very pleasant and most pleasing atmosphere, not of the cold formality and uneasy feeling as in the performance in Germany. The ballets received much response but there were three numbers of the divertissements which terminated the spectacle which simply brought down the house. These numbers were the *Swan* of Pavlowa, my *Persian Dance* and a *Polka of 1930* danced by Mlle. Plaskowieczka and Volinine.

Sketch of Tamara Swirskaya by the Russian artist A. Iacovleff.

What a pity that Pavlowa was more a dancer than a directress, as she could not stand to see other women dancers have laurels bestowed upon them. The Polka, which I had just seen danced for the first time, was also the last time it was presented on the program during my stay with her. I discovered it was a curious way to arrange the program in order to contra balance the chance of success of the dancers.

Clustine took the Gavotte for himself, and the Bacchanale which Pavley and I had worked on in Paris with the aim of dancing it with Pavlowa he (Clustine), without saying a word, gave the part to Mlle. de Swirskaya.

Mlle. de Swirskaya, although perfect in her solo dances "de plastique," was not the right choice for this. She had neither the abandon demanded for this dance nor the habit of dancing with partners employing the principles of the ballet; so it was rendered much less effectively than it could have been done. Pavlowa expressed to me her regret later at not dancing it with us, but Clustine, having given the part to Mlle. de Swirskaya, would bring no questioning of change. Even if she had, it would have caused difficulties with Mlle. Swirskaya, and again, Pavlowa had the habit of improvising and creating the dances which she wished to conserve for herself and would not take for herself a dance created by one of her dancers, but in case of too great a success she would suppress it as she had done with the Polka of Mlle. Plaskowieczka.

But this Bacchanale, anyhow, was one of the numbers that received the most applause and the best criticism. It was not deleted from the repertoire, but was rarely given, preferably in the towns of least importance or when an engagement was prolonged and they were short of numbers.

For the dance Hollandaise which Clustine had arranged for Pavley, he gave as partner Mlle. Kuhn, the premiere danseuse character, who had taken the place of Mlle. Gashewska. This dance was a great success and was copied everywhere in vaudeville by many dancers, but Pavlowa showed no jealousy because it was entirely out of her line of dancing, being a comic rural dance, danced in wooden shoes.

I was happy for Pavley that he had at least one new number in which he could make himself appreciated to the public, although it did not permit him to show himself to his best advantage and demonstrate all he could do, as he had the opportunity to do much later.

Our Return to the United States

THIS TIME we sailed on an English boat. It seemed so strange traveling at night, as we were compelled to have no light on the decks and the portholes closed, everything shielded for fear of the German submarines. Why should a boat carrying only civilians and going away from the place of conflict have cause to hold this fear of attack from an enemy only because this boat belonged to a certain country? It did seem like the world was retrograding—far different from the XVIII century when a French general in the language chivalrous could say, "English gentleman, you fire first." More recently, I remember my father recounting that in his youth, being in Odessa during the "Russo-Turque" war, from the time that the enemy disarmed they were considered as sacred and anyone would be labeled a scoundrel who attacked any of the disarmed. Some Turkish officers, who were taken prisoners, had been given lodgement in different families' homes and were treated is though they were guests.

Customs change and for a cycle we return to barbarism, citing the sinking of the Lusitania as an instance, and again the invasion of Belgium. It seemed horrible that they could invade Belgium, a neutral country. I was happy to leave for America, far from these hates which are cultivated by narrow-mindedness, or by commercial, socialistic and economical reasons.

The thought that we might be attacked and sunk did not worry me. In case of danger I am a fatalist. "Is life not an eternal danger? The risk many times is greater to continue to live."

Our Return to the United States

The voyage was uneventful, rather monotonous. To tour America again did not thrill me. It had no more the pleasure of adventure as of a place being seen for the first time. I was glad to be again in New York, and happy in the prospect of a sojourn in California, but I considered it a loss of time and a waste of my life, the time I spent in the towns of the Middle West.

The program this time was composed of the ballet of modern dances and of the *Puppen Fee,* followed, as was the custom, by the divertissements. As to *Puppen Fee,* I have an amusing experience to narrate about it.

This ballet was composed of two scenes. The first a botique of toys, and the second, the same place during the night after being transformed by the magic of the Fairy Doll, she having given life to all the automatons.

In the first scene I represented a comic poet; in the second a different character, and Clustine had inserted for me a special music for this number consisting of "Un pas de cinq".

Four dancers representing figurines of porcelain *de Saxe* occupied the four corners of the scene making all sorts of steps; my part was to occupy the center of the stage wearing a costume of the epoch of the ballets of Louis XIV, a Grecian costume in XVIII century spirit. It was all done in the spirit of the ballets of that time, I, paying my homages to the bergeres, presenting them with flowers.

This number could be appreciated by dancers or by balletomanes because it was very technical and very difficult, for it was done entirely on the toes. To the general public it did not appeal; it was a perfect flop and received but meagre applause, and that rather for politeness sake.

I was always disgusted at being obliged to execute this dance and was about to ask Clustine to cut it or to change it when that which I have to recount happened.

We arrived in a small town and had to dance in a theatre very badly equipped. There were few dressing rooms for the artists and the electric arrangement was such that when the lights were put out on the stage the dressing rooms also were plunged into darkness.

For the changing of the scene of the ballet *Puppen Fee* the light must be extinguished and so it was impossible for me to change my make-up of a grotesque poet and my costume and to be ready to personify the other person for this scene. I rushed for Clustine to ask what to do. He was very annoyed and most perplexed, not knowing how to work out of the situation. "With your consent," I said, "let me conserve the make-up and the costume of the poet." "But how can you do the other dance?" said he, much surprised. "It will be easy," I responded, "instead of making the dance serious and graciously, as you have arranged it, I will change nothing of the choreography, but I will change the character entirely and will make it grotesque and comic. There will be no risk in spoiling it for it never has obtained the favor of the public. We are in a small town and really it is all of very little importance." "All right," he said, "do as you wish."

As this arrangement had been made just at the last minute before the curtain lifted, nobody had been notified of the change, not even Pavlowa.

When the light is turned on in this second scene all the puppets are on the scene, and to the general consternation of the company they saw me in my costume of poet. Each asked himself how such a thing came to pass.

When the music began my dance, I executed it as I had explained to Clustine. I was in good humor, happy not to have to do it the usual way, which I had always abhorred. This way gave me the inspiration for improvisation.

The dancers, not having been forewarned and seeing my dance for the first time, could not control themselves or suppress their laughter.

I was stimulated by their support and by the fact the feeling that the public was reacting the same way, so I danced my best and it turned out a perfect success.

I believe that that was the time that I executed the dance the best. One of the dancers laughed so much that she had to quit the scene and go quickly and make a change, for to her had occurred an accident which ordinarily occurs only to babies.

The public applauded warmly. Pavlowa, who watched from the wings, laughed in bursts. As she danced in the following number, an *adagio* with Volinine, she many times, under pretense of flirting, turned her visage from the public so as to hide her laugh and gain control of her features.

I notice that I have always won my greatest success in the two extremes—the amusing and comic or the serious and tragic.

My confreres complimented me.

Monsieur Dandré laughed also and complimented me. However, for the next time he willed that I dance the part as formerly, saying that he believed that my way would take from the dignity of Pavlowa's spectacle. I danced it again two or three times according to the ancient fashion and with the same flat result. Then Monsieur Dandré reversed his decision. He realized that the ballet without my dance was more monotonous and had been losing its general success, so had me do it in the grotesque manner in one of the smaller towns to see again how it would affect the public. I did this and it had fine response. So he told me that decidedly it was not out of place and that I could continue to dance it that way.

The fact is the performance did gain by having something amusing introduced at this place. It was not a serious dance nor a triumph in any sense, but I felt satisfied to have changed a flop for a dance that pleased, and it all came about by a simple hazard of circumstances.

Even after I left Pavlowa they kept to my comic interpretation of the poet for those who succeeded me in that part, but I was told could not replace me.

Other Incidents

AT THE general rehearsal I was terribly disappointed when I saw for the first time the costumes which I had designed for the *Walpurgis Night,* I had not verified the making of them and I saw that they were very crudely put together, but Max Rabinoff, who was in the auditorium at the rehearsal, came back of the scenes, delighted with the coloring and the effect it gave in the dance when rendered by the ballet. I decided to go out in front and see for myself, and was surprised that the effect was as I had conceived it in the beginning and they were not bad. "The stage is a world created by the distance of perspective, combined with light effects, and everything has to be transposed in a certain key." Many times the true looks false and the false looks genuine. The real life and the stage are two separate worlds parallel in two different planes.

In the *Walpurgis Night,* I impersonated Mephisto and during a great part of the ballet I was with Pavlowa who, impersonating Helen of Troy, had been reclining on a couch for quite a long time. I always have been mystified by her double personality. A great dancer she was, but when not having much to do herself, as in the *Walpurgis Night,* she was principally concerned with nothing more than whether or not the house was full, even when smiling charmingly, as if acting her part. (That was her main thought.)

Among the dancers of the company were some with very childlike natures. One evening in Boston, having very little to do in the ballet of *Les Preludes de Liszt,* where I represented a bad spirit,

Other Incidents

I amused myself by making up like a ghost. I was waiting in the passageway near the loges when I met one of the Italian dancers. She gave a cry of terror. I thought she was joking but as I approached nearer to her to ask if she really thought my make-up well done, she almost had hysterics. I complimented myself on the success of my make-up, but could not conceive a nature so little developed. Many of them were of this calibre and it is quite natural that Pavley, Mlle. de Swirskaya and I formed a trio that was almost always together. Pavlowa did not fancy this.

Mlle. de Swirskaya had had great success with her dancing, but she did not outshine Pavlowa, her genre being entirely different, there was not cause for jealousy along that line, but this is the reason that Pavlowa was irritated. Pavlowa, who could be very elegant when she wished, often, when traveling and tired, would let herself go. One would never believe, seeing this little woman, seemingly thin, with hat pulled down over the eye, that it was the celebrated Pavlowa. On the contrary, Mlle. de Swirskaya was always attractive and often when arriving at a new theatre was taken for Pavlowa. Pavlowa, upon arriving at a theatre, would often be mistaken for one of the dancers or for a wardrobe woman.

So it was not a question of dancer against dancer, but woman against woman, which she could not tolerate.

Pavlowa let it be known that when the season terminated she would not re-engage Mlle. de Swirskaya, and Mlle. Swirskaya, just as independent and proud, let it be known that she would not accept a re-engagement and that the season had been for her just a fill-in during the time of the war.

The rivalry became a bit worse as the season wore on, particularly in New York and in Havana, because the taste of the New York public and the Cuban public was more advanced than that of the small and provincial towns of the United States. In Havana, not only woman to woman, but also as a dancer Mlle. Swirskaya rivalled Pavlowa. She danced the Oriental and the Greek dances in bare feet. Her dances were more musical and the choice of music

Other Incidents

better than Pavlowa's. Pavlowa, because of the shape of her feet, was debarred from dancing without sandals.

Clustine, knowing that Swirskaya was not a ballet dancer, gave her often to me for a partner, expecting by doing that to handicap many possibilities of execution, but if it was many times necessary to sacrifice technique, the musical artistic side was augmented. The dances reaching less to an effect and being less theatrical have, of course, less success in the provinces but obtain in reverse, more success in front of the elite and the connoisseur, where the number is much larger in the metropole and the Latin public. I was very happy to visit Cuba. I rather believe it is the reminiscence of my childhood spent in Nice that makes me adore the tropics. Havana, which I have seen again more recently, is presently a beautiful city. At that time it was not so large, but had a great charm and was very picturesque.

The public, cultured and most discriminative, was marvelous for me; they reminded me of the public of Europe which greeted me enthusiastically in Dresden, Berlin and London, or this one of New York which, at the Metropolitan, gave me such an ovation.

The Cubans choose their own favorites and exalt them with their bravos—those not to their liking are booed from the stage. In the United States the public, with the exception of that of New York and perhaps San Francisco and Los Angeles, accepts the artists imposed upon them by the management—by the press agent. It is not the talent or the genius of the artist that counts, but the manager who represents him and the publicity given in advance.

The Latin and European public create their star and select their favorite and place them on a pedestal; they also eliminate the bad and are not easily fooled. In the United States the artist doesn't count so much, it is the publicity; the money spent to present him is the principal thing that counts. If the artist has no real value the people come anyway to see him, without any protest; again, misrepresentation and without demonstration of disapproval. If the publicity is good, they will find in him even some quality; this will be for the manager next year to find a new zoo attraction. If

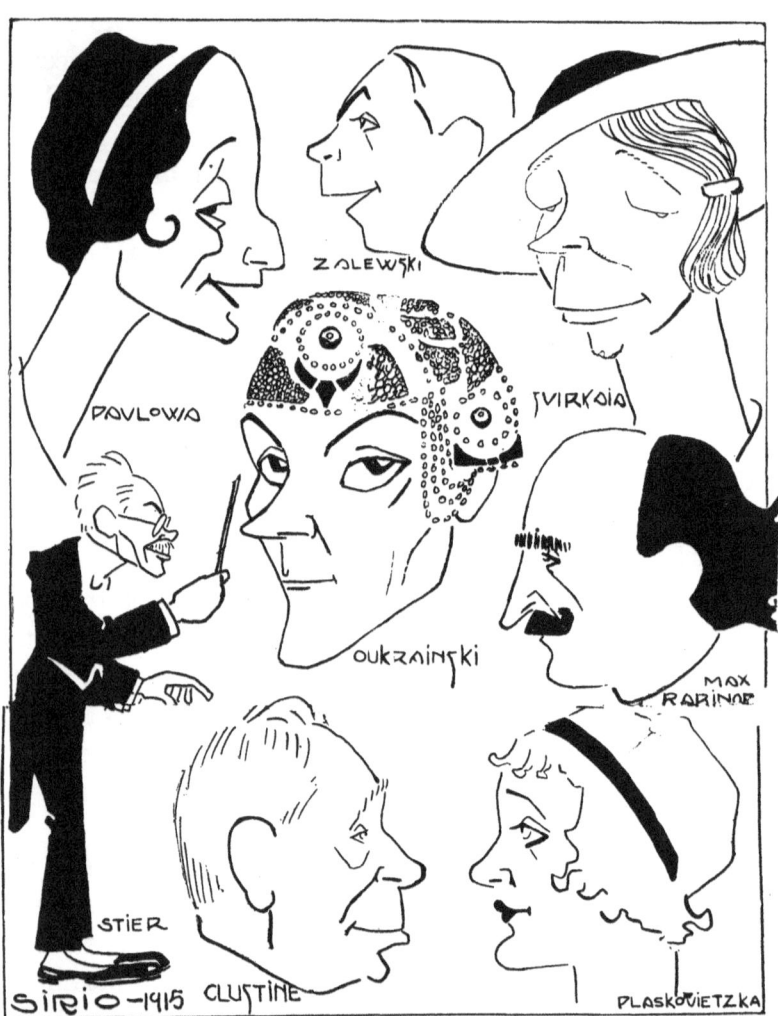

Caricature of Pavlowa Ballet in "El Figaro," Havana, Cuba.

Other Incidents

the artist is fair he is able to come back, but mostly in accordance with his publicity will his personal success be assured. There are generally three periods on tour: The first is a moderation of enthusiasm, fearing he is not very well known (in that case it is wiser not to praise him too much). Second, when he is known, admire everything that he does, admire the good and the bad, without discrimination, because the house was sold out, he must be good. Third period, really when the artist is at his pinnacle, having great experience and matured in his art, then they begin to criticize him, to give the impression to be blasé and to know what they are talking about, having seen or heard so many celebrities. This is really the spirit of the general public of the provincial town, and these poor people do not realize that they deprive themselves of the privilege to see the artist at his best because they are less receptive and are less demonstrative. An artist should be loved for his quality and for his defect, this makes his real personality. There is nothing on earth which is perfect; only mediocrity is uniform. This conception, I can say, makes the difference between the audiences of Europe, New York and places of Latin origin and the public of the towns in the United States.

On departing from the hotel leaving for Havana, Clustine had confided to Pavley the care of his valise while he went to buy a package of cigarettes. When he returned Pavley stopped to look after them and when the baggage arrived at the station Clustine's valise was not with it. We had to take the train in order not to miss the boat. So telegrams were sent and poor Clustine was in a nervous state, for the valise contained quite a sum of money and some jewels. It would have been only a worry to anyone else, but to Clustine it took fabulous proportions. Fortunately it was found before the boat set sail. One should have known Clustine to realize how comic or tragic this incident could have been.

On debarking at Havana a happening occurred which made me furious. Not speaking Spanish, I judged that it would be preferable to go with the company and so run no risk of getting lost or of

OTHER INCIDENTS

lodging too far from the theatre. They had equipages reserved for us, but instead of taking us directly to the hotel the management had given orders to pass and repass through the fashionable part of the city so that the inhabitants would know that a great theatrical company had come to town. This was most repellant to me. I recalled that in Russia, in that country, I had seen a circus arrive and parade around in that same fashion, so I felt that there was little dignity in making a like publicity for an organization like that of Pavlowa's. I thought it very indelicate also not to have spoken to the artists and to have obtained their authorization and their approbation as to their desire to be exhibited like that.

I was so humiliated that I was ready to quit, and I believe that I would have done so had I had a regular signed contract with Pavlowa, but this season, with the obsession of the war, I had only a verbal agreement with Monsieur Dandré which really gave me more advantages than the older signed contract, but I had given my word so I felt that I would have to keep it until the end.

I was well recompensed because my success in Havana was enormous. I appeared principally in the divertissements, in which I was permitted to show more of my modern genre than it was possible to do in the regular ballets of Pavlowa's repertoire.

In the ballets, Volinine served as Pavlowa's partner. Once his variation done he had the annoyance to act as a transfer man, carrying Pavlowa from one side of the stage to the other in the old adagio fashion of the old school of ballet from the Marinsky Imperial Theatre.

Volinine was always most particular in his work and most punctual, but one time, playing in a little town near Havana something occurred and he missed the train and we had to depart without him, so Clustine took it upon himself to act as his substitute. In the first ballet, *The Magic Flute,* the part should have been given to Constantin Kobeleff, who would have done very well, but no, Clustine must represent the young country boy in blonde peruque; it intensified his age and gave to him the aspect of a heavy old

OTHER INCIDENTS

woman such as one sees represented in caricatures. Happily, he did not dance the variation but only aided Pavlowa in her dancing.

In the *Walpurgis Night,* being Mephisto, I must be near Pavlowa, who was Helen; Volinine was her slave. When Clustine appeared in the costume of the slave, which was very brief, I had to bite my lips to keep from laughing aloud. The costume was composed of little straps which were woven over the chest: Volinine had a very well-proportioned body and this costume was most becoming to him, but when Clustine wore it the two narrow belts made the rolls of fat stand out, giving the effect of a stringed sausage or of the famous French poster of the *Michelin Tire*. This exhibition was worse than the appearance of the dancer T. The public could not help but laugh, too, and if the Spectacle passed without more of a demonstration it was for the reason that in this ballet the only real attraction was Pavlowa, she being perfect. Clustine's part was only incidental.

Clustine would have taken Volinine's part in the *Bacchanale,* too, but that would have been dancing vis-a-vis with Pavlowa, so she said that, having danced it already with Pavley, she would dance it with him again, so we were saved from that.

It was after this that I resolved to break with Pavlowa. I felt that it was no honor to dance with Pavlowa if she permitted such a thing at her performances, for in reality she was interested only in herself and not at all in her art. How could I persuade her to dance with me *La Peri* of Ducas when she had been feeling happy to execute the *Magic Flute* of Drigo? She interposed *Le Pizzicato de Silvia* by Delibes in almost all her ballets when she wished to have a personal success, and to save herself from fatigue, for this number was easy to execute for her. She decided to stage this ballet later and I was always under the impression she did it to make me regret having left her, as it was only when she saw that I would not return to her that she danced *La Peri*. She often spoke to me of "des Feuilles d'Automne," which she wished to dance with me to the music of Chopin. I was afraid this would be a repetition of the

OTHER INCIDENTS

Egytian dance or the Arensky Waltz and I began to be very skeptical of her prospects.

She said, too, that she would have my name put on the program as designer of the costumes in the *Walpurgis Night* and others, but Monsieur Dandré decided that as painter (artist) it would be preferable that I employ my own name instead of that of Oukrainsky. It seemed to me that it was to have less attention attracted to me.

I could see no future in staying with Pavlowa, only the possibility of falling into the bad taste of the banal and of the demoded conservative.

Pavley found himself in the same state of mind and with the further disadvantage of having less occasion to become known to the public. Mlle. Plaskowieczka felt the same, but feared to quit before being assured of another definite engagement. I would not have liked to have taken one of Pavlowa's dancers away from her. This was a secret to no one that Mlle. Swirskaya would not stay after the season was over.

I had an affection for Pavlowa and a great admiration for her as a dancer. It was only as directress that I criticize her.

So Pavley and I, having the same artistic aspirations and the same reasons of discontent about the repertoire, found it quite natural to later join up professionally.

I left Havana with great regret. Pavlowa was delighted to go. Her success had been great, but it was not absolutely all her own; others had shared in it. The expense of the trip, too, was very high; she just broke even and this did not please her either.

On our return to the United States we stopped over in a very small town to break the route. The theatre was small and very old, without dressing room for the artists. We had to dress ourselves in our rooms at the hotel and pass by a lane to the theatre. Of all the places that I had danced with Pavlowa it surely was the smallest. A contrast, surely, to that in Germany where we danced for the Kaiser Wilhelm II or to the gala performance in London with the Queen present.

Other Incidents

The balcony, according to the custom of the Southern states, was reserved exclusively for the Negroes. It was the first time that I had seen Pavlowa appear under such circumstances. I had no prejudice against the black race and if the hall had been entirely composed of them I would not have cared, but it was this separation which made it evident that one part of the public seemed to be considered inferior to the other, and in this old, dirty theatre it gave the aspect of what they call, in America, a burlesque house. I believe that ordinarily it was shows of this kind (burlesque) that filled this theatre and this must have been the first time that a great artist appeared there.

I smiled ironically at the difference of what life really is and the dreams that one has of it. I would never have imagined that a world celebrity would be obliged to perform under such aspects.

In starting out with Pavlowa I had believed that we would appear only in the capitals, the larger and important cities during the best seasons, and only presenting the best creation from the viewpoint of the music of the choreography and of the scenery. We had done that in London and in Germany, but now we were most certainly at the other extreme. On the artistic side, it was rarely that I had seen performances given of great merit; ordinarily, it was the banal camouflaged by the genius of Pavlowa who made it appear to have some merit.

Diaghilew's method had been to search for the new—to assemble the artists, to make and develop the creations to their best. After this was the tactic to surprise the *bourgeois,* a pose to admire the grotesque and to impose this taste to snobbishness which follow him, fearing to pass as ignorant.

Pavlowa was commercial. She used her art to flatter the taste of the big public and, above all, to star herself. Happily for me, we could not keep on traveling continuously; we had a season, a month, at the Century Theatre in New York. This theatre was a house which truly had the air of being one, something seldom seen in the States; that is perhaps the reason why it has since been demolished.

Pavlowa with a partner in the ballet "La Peri" by Paul Dukas.
Bronz by Malvina Hoffman.

Other Incidents

Its proportions were perfect. It had a stage large enough to present all that one could wish, and not too large for right perspective for the human eye; opera glasses were sufficient to admire great artists but it was not necessary to use a telescope.

We had an excellent season and, needing a varied repertoire, Pavlowa was forced to present some of her really beautiful ballets, and not only the commercial ones.

Les Preludes of Liszt with his music choreographed by Michel Fokine, and decorations and costumes by Boris Anisfeld.

Oriental Fantasy, although with a pot-pouri as to music, had the beautiful decorations and costumes of Leon Bakst and a good choreography by Zaylich.

The Walpurgis Night, with music of Gounod, costumes that I had designed, a scenery passable, and an acceptable choreography by Clustine.

Chopiniana on the suave and romantic music of Chopin well orchestrated by Glasounow, having very beautiful scenery and costumes of the conventional ballet, and a choreography by Clustine rather banal but well arranged.

Giselle, the old ballet of Adam, but which with *Coppelia* by Delibes can be classed as standard classic ballets. These two ballets in their line rank with the traditional operas such as *Aida* or *Traviata*.

These ballets mentioned were those which I considered good or acceptable among those Pavlowa presented, as against those others which I considered commercial and inexcusable.

The Magic Flute by Drigo, choreography by Petipa, simple and a rural banality of a preceding generation, music insipid, decor and costume most conventional and interesting.

It was the same with the ballet *La Fille Mal Gardée*, and *Le Retour de La Cavalerie* and a ballet, horror of horrors with music of a circus and the French Children Ronde "J'ai du bon tabac dans ma tabatiere". This ballet was *Paquita*, with a Spanish *Pas de Quatre* on toe, with all the bad taste of the precedent generation of the time of the decadence of the ballet. There was also the "Le Reveil

Program cover of Pavlowa Ballet, Century Opera House, New York City.

Other Incidents

de Flore," a Greek ballet—on the toes—an oldster disguised under an aspect of modernism—badly done.

Raimonda, another ancient banality, although it had the music of Glasounow.

Invitation to the Dance, bad interpretation of this music which we so well rendered as *Le Spectre de la Rose.*

Le Ballet des Dances Moderne, foolish both choreographically and musically.

Fairy Doll, a Viennese ballet—good for a place like a Hippodrome, but absolutely out of place on a concert stage.

It is certain that America owes to Pavlowa the presentation of the first beautiful ballets with scenery and costumes and music by the great masters. The dance, through her, has been rendered more popular and has become more appreciated by the American public. But again, they can reproach her that through her egotism and her desire for personal and financial success she passed off on them much that was banal and passé.

The dance also could reproach her for her retrograde as she developed and for presenting from only time to time, really against her wish, some modern conceptions in order not to stay too far away from Diaghilew.

The last ballets enumerated were those which Pavlowa presented during the two years that I stayed with her.

Later, she presented *Autumn Leaves*. She danced this ballet with Volinine. She decided to show the ballet *La Peri* which I had counseled her so often to put on her program. She danced it with a dancer, Stowitz; he also designed the costumes and the scenery for her later on.

When I severed my connections with them Monsieur Dandré engaged an American dancer to take my place. His name was Beli Bene, also a designer. Monsieur Dandré took the attitude that he could replace me right away with a designer-dancer. Bene stayed with Pavlowa a short time and then I heard no more about him.

Other Incidents.

In our season in New York the public showed great enthusiasm in my regard.

I met a very charming woman, a sculptress of renown, Malvina Hoffman, who asked if she could make some sketches of me. She told me of things which gave me great pleasure; being in Paris, she had shown some photographs of myself to the celebrated Rodin; he suggested to her to make sketches of me and told her, "this one is very advanced in his art, and most interesting." This compliment, coming from such an artist as Rodin, whom I did not personally know, had truly great value.

She worked on a frieze that she had commenced of Pavlowa and Mordkin in the Bacchanale in which they had danced together, but the work was interrupted by the disagreement between the two.

Pavlowa posed for her sometimes between performances and asked Pavley to pose with her, for she found him the most perfect for the attitudes—the movements—although she had rarely given him an opportunity to demonstrate this on the stage. I believe the principal reason was because Pavley was so much younger than she and so she might not show to the best of her advantage.

Of all the celebrated dancers, Duncan was the only one who escaped the adverse criticism of Pavlowa, who had a true and sincere admiration for her, perhaps because their art was so different, but this was no condescendence of Pavlowa who had always a word of encouragement for the mediocre but a sarcasm for the great.

One day, seeing Pavlowa, after some years had passed, I complimented her on her attitude in the ballet d'Orphé, where truly she had been excessively beautiful. She said, "I gave of my best. It is much different than I danced ordinarily; I endeavored to recall what I had seen Isadora Duncan do." Pavlowa, this time, however, did not estimate herself at her true value. Perhaps, naively, she did believe that she had copied Duncan, but Duncan could have been no more than an inspiration; Pavlowa could not copy, but with the force of her personality she had made a creation most beautiful and personal to herself.

OTHER INCIDENTS.

At the close of the New York season Pavlowa was much embarrassed as to what to do with the company, the tour being at an end. She could not return to London as she had thought at first, for the war continued, and yet the summer was not the season to stay in the United States.

Incense burner by Malvina Hoffman, representing Serge Oukrainsky in the ballet Oriental Fantasy. Back view.

Incense burner by Malvina Hoffman, representing Serge Oukrainsky in the ballet Oriental Fantasy. Front view.

Midway Garden

THE SITUATION in general was embarrassing to Pavlowa. She had the habit of giving two months vacation to the members of her organization and to have them the rest of the time with her, guaranteeing them to be occupied. It was too early to interrupt the season; it would be too enormous an undertaking to take the company to Europe and bring them back again later to the United States.

Even a season in the United States seemed a great risk, for announcements had been made with great ballyhoo of the Diaghilew company coming for the first time to the United States. Pavlowa resented and feared this rivalry. She knew that she was a favorite with the public and from the point of view of the dance had nothing to fear; it was all to her advantage. But she realized that Diaghilew's repertoire was more advanced and more artistic than hers.

Her aim was basically to popularize herself personally and to make a commercial success by catering to the taste of the great public rather than to that of the connoisseurs. Diaghilew, on the contrary, had all his expenses guaranteed so was freed of the money worry and could give free vent to his artistic conceptions.

It was said that Otto Kahn was bringing the Russian Ballet of Diaghilew with this tremendous advertising for the purpose to flood the Wall Street market with paper of Russian loans. It was very secondary what the ballet could bring in box office returns, in comparison with the enormous benefits the transaction of Wall Street could procure, stimulating the public interest on everything Russian.

Midway Garden

The Diaghilew tour was less an artistic undertaking than a financial propaganda of Wall Street, and the deficit assumed by the Metropolitan.

Pavlowa, on the contrary, had to conserve and balance her budget; though she made much, she had heavy expenses which she could not allow to get out of control. Her orchestra, for example, of twenty musicians (increased in number in the larger cities to something like forty) could not compare with Diaghilew's (he used about eighty). He presented the very latest, which, aside from their choreographic interest, were at the same time ballets of merit and musically novelties. He had Nijinsky, Fokine, Karsavina, Ida Rubinstein, Nijinskaya, none of whom had ever been in the United States, and so made a great appeal to the American public, a public always in quest, and not of being faithful to its old favorites as do, above all, the public of England.

So Diaghilew had all this on his side—the more brilliant ballets, the superior music, the newness of presentation, the freedom from financial worries, fabulous publicity, the advantage of pushing to the front different artists (Pavlowa guarded this privilege jealously for herself alone).

The situation distressed Pavlowa and Monsieur Dandré.

Nobody could foretell, however, how things were to be. To foresee that the season of 1915-1916 was to be disastrous for all.

Different rumors were circulated in the company, but at last Pavlowa announced officially that the following season she planned to have a double organization. It would consist of a troupe half ballet and half opera—"The Boston Opera and Anna Pavlowa with her Russian Ballet."

I felicitated myself on having taken the decision to quit Pavlowa. With her organization of the dance alone it was so difficult to make one's self known, she, not bringing her dancers to the front; joined to an opera there would be still less opportunity and interest.

Pavlowa and Monsieur Dandré desired us (Pavley and me) to stay with them and made a very advantageous proposition to us, better salaries during the season and many promises for the future when they would be detached from the opera company.

I felt that Pavlowa had a double interest in wishing us to remain; one was on the side of the artisticness of the Spectacle—the subject of designs for the costumes (which I made) and my opinion in conversation, and our dances; the other was that she would love to have seen defeat in our plan of joining up with Mlle. de Swirskaya, whom she believed responsible for our desire to part.

Such was the situation when suddenly Pavlowa announced that to finish the season she had accepted for the summer an engagement in Chicago in the Midway Garden. This announcement had a double effect on the company. The dancers receiving only a modest salary and not having any personal fortune to permit them to remain at leisure were content to know that they would have work for the summer, but were displeased at the engagement she had accepted.

In America, the principal aim is the gain, and if one is well paid the engagement itself is of little importance. In Europe, the artists have a certain discrimination in the choice of their engagements (at least they did in those times).

Pavlowa had never appeared with her ballet but in Spectacles of the highest order, concerts, operas, galas.

The Midway Garden was a summer restaurant in the open air with a stage before which there were some seats for the spectators, the rest of the Garden being filled with tables where people ate and at the same time saw the presentation. The feeling in the company was as though Pavlowa had lost her prestige by accepting this engagement in a cabaret.

Personally, I much admired her for having condescended to appear under such conditions in order to save the situation, and so keep her company with her. We soon left for Chicago, where we had to spend the summer.

Pavlowa also obtained a film contract; she was to make scenes portraying the history of *The Dumb Girl of Portici*.

During the engagement at the Midway Garden, between the

Pavlowa in the file "The Dumb Girl of Portici". Pavlowa lower left on floor.

acts Pavlowa did some scenes of this film. She was to complete it in Hollywood at the end of the Chicago season before going into the ballets and operas undertakings.

Pavley, Mlle. de Swirskaya and I stayed at the Hotel del Prado, which was not far from the Midway Garden. There we commenced to create a repertoire for our future use.

During our spare time (our performances were generally in the evening) we gave lessons, many persons requesting us to do so. It proved to be the beginning of our school which developed later in Chicago, but we had started in with the idea of making a little capital to pay for the costumes and other things necessary for our presentations.

We had much success at the Midway Garden and were very optimistic as to the success of our future plans.

As it was a long season in Chicago, Pavlowa had need to add to her repertoire, so decided to give *Raimonda* by Glazounow. This ballet again was of the old school, inconceivably demoded. Pavlowa represented a princess of the middle age, but she dressed herself anyway in a short tarlatan and in this outfit she settled herself on the throne and gave audience to Knights and Saracens in her tarlatan of 1880. This is according to the artistic tradition of the Imperial Russian Ballet of the Marinsky Theatre of epoch pre-Diaghilew.

Pavlowa tried to dissuade me from quitting, and I had my regrets for I admired her art and would prefered to have stayed with her for, in spite of her personal faults, of her professional jealousy, I liked her well and I realized and appreciated that it was she who gave me my first opportunity. But seeing again such a presentation as this, I was reenforced in my decision to part from her.

However, our separation was to be one only of absence during her season of opera. It was understood that we would rejoin her later, that Pavley, and I would return in the Springtime for the season in London, that we were to be absent only for the winter when she had truly no need of our services. Pavlowa, nevertheless, insisted

Midway Garden

still more that we stay with her, especially after the following incident.

The Spectacles of the Midway Garden were given in the open air on a stage, as I described previously, but if it rained they were given in a building adjoining in the hall of the restaurant on the floor, with the tables and diners all around. Volinine categorically refused to appear under such conditions. He said that on the stage with the footlights between him and the public he considered himself an artist demonstrating his art to a public coming to admire and showing their admiration by their applause, but to dance in the midst of tables where the people were engrossed in eating was much different; there, dining was their principal interest and one was only a distraction, and that appearing under such conditions one was no more an artist but a servant on a par with the waiters in the restaurant.

In 1915 one could not envisage that, twenty years later the debutantes of New York would launch a mode to appear as the attractions in the night clubs.

Consequently, Pavlowa found herself without a partner in the dances she had with him. She asked me if I would, in addition to my own dances with her, consent to replace Volinine in those that he had with her.

I felt sorry to see an artist like Pavlowa placed in such a position. It was no more agreeable to me than it was to Volinine to dance in a restaurant in the midst of tables, but as I was appearing under a pseudonym, it gave me more freedom. I considered that if so great an artist as Pavlowa could permit herself to do so, I could see no reason why I should refuse. I consented to replace Volinine under the circumstances and so save Pavlowa from embarrassment.

As this establishment was not arranged for such Spectacles, Pavlowa and all the dancers had to make their changes in the toilettes of the restaurant. It pained me to see such a great artist reduced to such circumstances for the necessity of making money. It was no

Midway Garden

disgrace to do so, but surely it was a decided contrast to her gala performances of London and Germany.

During our stay in Chicago, Mlle. de Swirskaya, Pavley and I endeavored to procure engagements for the following winter. The Lake View Musical Society of Chicago engaged us for a performance to take place in Orchestra Hall. A manager from Indianapolis, Ona B. Talbot, who had had previous business affairs with Mlle. de Swirskaya, engaged us to organize a festival in that city. We hoped to obtain other engagements through it.

I thought that all would go well with us through the winter and that we would rejoin Pavlowa in London in the Springtime as planned. In case things would not turn out like we had been expecting, Pavley and I could return anyway to London to wait there for Pavlowa. We could also give a few performances there and if everything turned for the worse my father could send me some money, because for the last two years I had not drawn a cent from him, and this could have temporarily straightened out my business. We certainly did not expect the following event to happen, to find ourselves without engagements, to have the Bolshevism explode in Russia, which ruined my father entirely. Pavlowa not to have her season in London, and to find ourselves temporarily penniless. All these events which had to happen to me will be the subject of my next book (My Nine Years as Ballet Master for the Chicago Grand Opera).

But to return to the Midway Garden—the season passed without incident except for one fact that annoys me greatly. Miss Van Buren, who wrote for the American Journal, demanded an interview for an article which she desired to write on my success in the Midway Garden. This article not appearing after a proper lapse of time, I asked her the reason of the delay. She told me that Monsieur Dandré had said that they preferred to have no public attention drawn to the artists who were leaving the Pavlowa organization, so the article did not appear. I thought it rather a small thing to do. Although the incident was not of great importance, it made me recall

Midway Garden

how at Atlantic City, coming from the stage, after my *Persian Dance* had called forth a veritable ovation, Pavlowa, who had had but one recall after her *Swan,* said to me, "One must have real genius to enthuse such audiences." But it was said in a tone which left me without a doubt as to its ironic intent. It was unkind of her for she reaped great triumphs the greater part of the time, so why hurt herself by begrudging others success?

I had never given an encore during all the time that I was with her, for I would not wound her exaggerated sensitiveness. The last evening of the engagement at the Midway Garden was to be the last time that I was to dance with Pavlowa. I had, as was usual, a great ovation after my dance done in bare feet and on the toes—which I alone can do. After recall and recall I demanded of the leader of the orchestra, Monsieur Stier, to repeat the music. He was much surprised, looked at me in astonishment and repeated the number as requested.

I had the satisfaction of giving this encore the last time that I danced with Pavlowa and terminated my engagement with cheers and bravos. It was not so much the fact of showing to Pavlowa the dancer she would lose, but it was done, above all, with the aim of preventing them from saying that my departure was due to the fact that my work was not up to par or that my success had diminished.

Separations

It was finished, the season terminated. Pavley and I must go to Pavlowa to make our adieu and receive our contract for rejoining her in London in the Springtime.

Monsieur Dandré received us alone, according to his custom when business was to be discussed, and, as always, was very amiable. We spoke of one thing and another and then brought up the subject of the contract. He then announced that Pavlowa, after reflecting, was opposed to giving us a signed contract for the Springtime if we quitted her. He tried hard to dissuade us from parting, using many arguments, making our future look very dark. He repeated her advantageous offers.

At last he said that she did not desire to have a contract obliging us to return to her, for our affairs might be going well, but that if things turned out badly for us she would be happy to have us return.

To these words I replied that I had much admiration for Madame Pavlowa (which was true) and that even if things went very well I would be very happy to return to dance with her, but if things went badly I would have too much dignity to return, and would rather try to change professions.

At this response Monsieur Dandré said that we had better talk directly to Pavlowa on the subject. He passed into the next room, where he talked for some time with her. She finally came to us and, taking on a maternal air (which I had seen her use on other occa-

Serge Oukrainsky in his Persian Dance.

sions), she told us that we must listen to someone with experience and take her advice and not leave.

She said that we could not realize all the worries that we would have and that we would regret the parting and long for the time free from care that we would enjoy with her.

With the inexperience of youth we did not really grasp that she was right.

Knowing how to play on our vanity, she said that we could not hope to obtain engagements as with her; that we might get an act in vaudeville dancing before a mediocre public, but not before a choice audience of concert and opera goers. That we could not dream of getting engagements as with her, seeing that we were just commencing, were unknown, while she had already a reputation universally known.

Nobody could read the future and know that we were to have the same engagements as she; that I was to be Master of the Ballets of the Chicago Grand Opera Company and that in 1922 we were to create, Pavley and I, the first American Ballet which, under the name of Pavley-Oukrainsky Ballet, was to be a company of the same size as her own. It was to give gala performances before the Prince of Italy, Huberto of Savoy, at the Theatre Colon of Buenos Aires, and was to appear before the Queen of Rumania in the Auditorium at Chicago—gala performances like we had had with her.

But this fashion of talk had an antagonistic effect on Pavley and on me. We felt that if she so doubted us she did not value us at our true worth. We would prove that we were capable.

At last both of us got the impression that it was not her fear of having a contract with us forcing us to return to her after great success, but on the contrary, knowing the condition of business, she knew how difficult it was to succeed no matter how great the talent one must have, and she was persuaded that we would be forced to return to her with bowed heads after our many failures. Speaking with much indulgence, we could sense that she expected such an event and believed she still could gain more prestige in our eyes if things happened that way.

The loss of the London season, which never happened, was what I regretted most; but we were unalterable in our decision as was Pavlowa in hers. We left, both sides wishing success to the other, for the winter with a hope of a reunion in the Springtime. So opened a new page in life for Pavley and me. We were now on our own.

Independent

I WILL not linger on the events which followed. They were numberless.

I will recount only the things which happened immediately after our separation and the contacts I had on different occasions with Pavlowa.

The year 1916 was unlucky for all. After our two or three engagements we could find no others which would satisfy us, so again we gave lessons for our subsistence, and founded the Pavley-Oukrainsky Ballet School in Chicago.

Diaghilew had arrived in America, but under adverse circumstances. In spite of the fact that he had all expenses guaranteed, enormous sums of money for his Spectacles and colossal publicity, he had not Nijinsky with him. He (Nijinsky) was held a prisoner of war in Austria-Hungary. To fill his place Diaghilew had a new protége, Léonide Massine, whom he was pushing to the front.

For his debut Diaghilew presented in Paris *Legende de Joseph,* a ballet with music by Richard Strauss and setting by Bakst. Joseph was danced by Massine and the role of Madame Potiphar by Ida Rubenstein. She had hoped that Nijinsky would be free to fill the Joseph role; to appear with an unknown did not please her. Some disputes occurred and Ida Rubenstein was reported ill and her relations with Diaghilew were broken. Diaghilew gave that part to the prima-dona Maria Kousnezoff to appear with Massine. Michel Fokine

Andreas Pavley as the Harlequin in "Rondo Capriccioso" by Saint-Saens.

and his wife, Fokina, had quitted also. Karsavina had married in England and deserted him, too.

Diaghilew, arriving in America, had none of his stars with him, neither Pavlowa, Kschesinska, Karsavina, Ida Rubinstein, Fokina, Nijinskaya, Estaphieva or Piltz as ballerinas, nor Michel Fokine, Nijinsky, Mordkin or Volinine as dancers. Adolph Bolm was the only exception. Bolm he had elevated to the title of Master of the Ballet, he who formerly danced only the character roles and the mimes.

The difficult work of the classic dancing was confided to Vladimirow. The publicity was especially centered on Bolm, he was the only one of the old stars, and on Massine, who was a beginner at the time, being Diaghilew's protége. Diaghilew had the intention of advancing him to take the place of Nijinsky in the minds of the public.

It was under these conditions that Diaghilew opened his Spectacles in New York, having as principal ballerina a premiere dancer of Russia whose name I have forgotten. The American public, accustomed to the exquisite finesse of Pavlowa, did not take to her and Diaghilew, realizing that she had not produced a favorable impression, he had her return to Europe.

To take her place he immediately engaged Lopouchowa, a very good dancer, but she had just terminated a tour of vaudeville and had everywhere appeared at popular prices.

Diaghilew's prices were above those that the public had been accustomed to pay to see Pavlowa dance. They had been raised to those of the Grand Opera, and, not producing the stars that had been heralded, the result was pitiful; the theatres were almost empty.

Madame Kellogg Fairbank, a society woman of Chicago who patronized the ballet, prayed me to make a speech at a club to interest the public in this enterprise.

In this first tour of the United States, Diaghilew made a terrible flop, suffered a terrible loss. It would have been ruination to him had he been responsible for the expenses of the Spectacle.

The next year was better for him, for he then had Nijinsky in his company. The prices were lessened and often the performances were given in smaller theatres and the orchestra reduced.

Nijinsky, in America, had not the opportunity of showing at his best, for, with the exception of *Till Eulenspiegel,* all the repertoire had been already presented. Pavlowa was also unlucky. She chose to show for the Boston Opera *The Dumb Girl of Portici,* as she had done for the films. She had chosen this one for the reason that the principal personage in it was a mime. This work had been especially written for the celebrated danseuse and mime, La Tzoucci, who excelled in technique and mimicry.

Later, seeing Pavlowa in Chicago in her dressing room, she expressed a deep regret at not being able to report a success in this role. "After all, perhaps I am only a dancer," she said.

Pavlowa was disparaging herself! She was surely an excessively good mime as well as a ballerina, but this opera of the *Muette de Portici* was demoded, a libretto which did not interest people of present times. The music was mediocre and the public was disappointed because it wanted to see her dance, which she did not do.

The combination of opera and ballet resulted in doubling the expenses of the organization and to decrease the interest of the dance public to over half.

"This year," Pavlowa said to me, "it is not I who am the star, it is Tamaka Miuri."

Tamaka Miuri was the first Japanese woman to sing the role of *Madame Butterfly* in the opera of that name. It was included in the repertoire of the Boston Opera. She was truly a great artist and rendered a perfect interpretation of this character.

Pavlowa recognized the value of Tamaka Miuri to the company as a financial draw, even though it displeased her that she, herself, was forced to take a secondary position. It was a case of the business woman who was Pavlowa consoling the artist child who was also Pavlowa. The season of the Boston Opera terminated with a loss and Pavlowa did not try a similar undertaking the following season.

Independent

Although this next season was financially better it did not bring her more success. She did not return to London in the Springtime, so neither did we.

Fearing again the competition of the Diaghilew ballets in spite of his defeat of the year before, but knowing that this time Diaghilew would have Nijinsky with him, she accepted an engagement at the Hippodrome in New York. There, again, she made the mistake of resurrecting one of the old ballets, *Sleeping Beauty* by Tschaikowsky.

The audience of the Marinsky Theatre of St. Petersburg could stand a ballet of three acts as could the public of China stand plays running many weeks. The American public, loving speed to an excess, has more the spirit of the advanced capitals of Europe than that of the Asiatic spirit of St. Petersburg. Diaghilew catered to this impatient and alert demand of London, Paris, and Berlin, but Pavlowa, though going to great expense in the staging of this ballet (using setting and costumes by Bakst and exerting her own great genius), could not surmount the insipid monotony of the long dances and the management requested her to make a change. She gave a series of divertissements that would appeal to the popular vaudeville taste.

Then by a Machiavelien quirk of fate Charlotte, the ice skater, was engaged at the Hippodrome. She was a true human phenomenon —skating on ice, she did all that Pavlowa did on her toes. The lines were noticeably less beautiful and there was much less of art; it was purely acrobatic skating. For a public such as that which patronized the Hippodrome with Pavlowa showing between an act of comedians and that of trained elephants, Charlotte appeared the more remarkable.

After these two years of failures, Pavlowa did not return to the United States for two years. She then returned under the management of Fortune Gallo, and this tour was for her a veritable triumph; a triumph which she greatly merited. Each year, however, her company became more feeble, the dancers recruited were inferior but, by contrast, the repertoire became more modern and a little better.

[191]

Tamara Swirskaya in one of her terpsichorean interpretations, "The Birth of Venus".

Independent

Pavlowa then took a trip around the world and later staged a ballet depicting her *Oriental Impressions*. It was very interesting.

She at last decided to give *La Peri*, which, though conceived without symbolism or mysticism, was at least a beautiful work musically. *The Autumn Leaves* which she also gave had a decidedly artistic side.

Pavlowa had little choreographic sense in spite of her incomparable execution, however, she created her *Dragonfly*, which was a simple marvel, and in which she only could personify the name part as she did in that of the *Cygne*.

I had a few occasions to correspond with Monsieur Dandré about rejoining Pavlowa in dancing. It was principally about touring in South America, and neither Pavley nor I were desirous of going there. We were only interested in a chance to go to London. But fate willed that we were not to go back there. Although we always remained on very good terms with Pavlowa and Monsieur Dandré, I was told that she harbored a resentment because of our leaving. Soon after our departure she changed the costumes of *The Gavotte* because they were designed by me. She had others made but the dance lost all of its success by the change and she was obliged to return to those that I had created for her.

She would not recognize that Pavley and I had made great success after leaving her.

I do not know whether or not it is true, but we were told that in Chicago Pavlowa came to one of the matinees to see the ballet that we had staged for the Chicago Opera, but that she did not show herself in public, surveying the performance from behind a curtain in one of the loges, not letting us know that she had come to judge of the success that we had made.

Some time later, after one of her performances in Paris, given at the Trocadero, I went to her to compliment her as I always did when in a city where she appeared. Bakst was in her dressing room; I would so have loved to have made his acquaintance, but

The five ballet positions executed by Serge Oukrainsky.

instead of presenting us to each other, she so maneuvered it that we were not introduced.

However, in spite of our fine engagements, after leaving her we often regretted the loss of the happy days and the freedom from worry. She was right when she warned us the satisfaction and success of recognition by the public did not balance all the troubles and the worries of the responsibilities of big enterprises. Perhaps those two years passed with Pavlowa were embellished with the illusions of youth. Those little questions of professional jealousy were not truly of great importance in comparison with all the good that being with her did for me in giving me the opportunity to develop myself.

No one can be perfect, so in spite of her genius Pavlowa was at the same time human and consequently subject to defects and faults. These small imperfections of hers are excusable, for without them she would without doubt, have been less of a personality, imperfect in her art. Personally, I have always liked and admired Pavlowa and am thankful to her for introducing me to the public. I have written in this book the facts as they have happened. This in point of view of the authenticity of the events, of the psychology of her personality which I have written, but I do not like to reproach her, her pride which was like I say, pure childishness. It was her ardent devotion to her art which made her place herself apart as an apostle of the dance demanding to receive, exclusively, all the adulation.

Pavlowa often said that she would retire to Aize on the Riviera when through with public life, but she would never have been happy unoccupied and far from the theatre.

With the bad taste which developed during the war and the post-war time she and her art would have been smothered by the miasma of its crude realities.

So she passed away in the perfection of her art at the pinnacle of her career, brilliant, artistic, light, immaculate, like the downy whiteness of her *Swan*. When Atropos severed the thread of her life, it was the hand of Terpsichore herself which clipped the delicate flower who was Pavlowa, which had kept in her calyx the suave aroma of the absolute perfection before the petals would fade.

She died in Holland; I was greatly grieved when I heard of it. It seemed as if a little of myself had passed with her. She was the material witness of the first dream of my youth. Pavlowa is no more. No! This is not a reality, only her material incarnation has passed away. Pavlowa is here, because Pavlowa is immortal. She still vibrates in the spirit of all who have known her and this vibration will continue in the spirit of generations, to future generations. It is the wave of the art of the Dance, moved by the passage of the *Swan;* they are the circle of this limpid ether which grows larger and spreads out in the eternity of remembrances.

There have been other celebrated and seductive danseuses, Camargo, Taglione, Tzouki, Karsavina and others, but there has been but one soul beautiful, incomparable, inimitable *Swan*—Pavlowa.

Hollywood, 1940.

In Preparation
'My Nine Years with the Chicago Grand Opera'

www.ingramcontent.com/pod-product-compliance
Lightning Source LLC
Chambersburg PA
CBHW021101080526
44587CB00010B/330